# CLOUD-BASED CI/CD FOR SOFTWARE TEAMS

# Cloud-Based CI/CD for Software Teams

RAFEAL MECHLORE

Readers Publications

# Contents

| | |
|---|---:|
| INDEX | 1 |
| INTRODUCTION | 3 |
| Chapter 1 | 23 |
| Chapter 2 | 41 |
| Chapter 3 | 61 |
| Chapter 4 | 78 |
| Chapter 5 | 101 |
| Chapter 6 | 120 |
| Chapter 7 | 137 |
| Chapter 8 | 154 |
| Chapter 9 | 173 |

# INDEX

Introduction

1. Definition of Cloud-Based CI/CD
2. Importance of CI/CD in Modern Software Development
3. Purpose and Scope of the Book
4. Target Audience
5. Overview of the Book's Structure

Chapter 1 :Fundamentals of CI/CD
1.1 What Is CI/CD?
1.2 Benefits of CI/CD
1.3 Key Principles and Concepts
1.4 CI/CD Workflow Overview

Chapter 2 :Cloud Infrastructure for CI/CD
2.1 Understanding Cloud Services
2.2 Choosing the Right Cloud Provider
2.3 Setting Up Cloud Environments for CI/CD
2.4 Cost Considerations and Optimization

Chapter 3 :Designing CI/CD Pipelines in the Cloud
3.1 Building Blocks of CI/CD Pipelines
3.2 Best Practices for CI/CD Pipeline Design
3.3 Implementing Infrastructure as Code (IaC)
3.4 Handling Code Repositories and Version Control

Chapter 4 :Automated Testing in CI/CD
4.1 Types of Testing in CI/CD

4.2 Integrating Testing Tools with CI/CD Pipelines
4.3 Ensuring Test Coverage and Quality
4.4 Test Automation Strategies

## Chapter 5 : Continuous Integration in the Cloud
5.1 Setting Up CI Environments
5.2 Triggering Builds and Tests
5.3 Handling Build Artifacts
5.4 CI/CD Security Best Practices

## Chapter 6 : Continuous Deployment in the Cloud
6.1 Configuring CD Environments
6.2 Deploying Applications Automatically
6.3 Managing Rollbacks and Roll-forwards
6.4 Monitoring Deployed Applications

## Chapter 7 : Advanced CI/CD Topics
7.1 Blue/Green Deployments
7.2 Canary Releases
7.3 Containerization and Orchestration
7.4 Scalability and Performance Considerations

## Chapter 8 : Security in Cloud-Based CI/CD
8.1 Security Challenges in CI/CD Pipelines
8.2 Implementing Security Scans and Checks
8.3 Compliance and Governance
8.4 Secrets Management and Access Control

## Chapter 9 : Best Practices and Tips
9.1 Lessons Learned from Successful Implementations
9.2 Common Pitfalls to Avoid
9.3 Tips for Continuous Improvement
9.4 Future Trends in Cloud-Based CI/CD

# INTRODUCTION

Because software creation is changing so quickly, it has never been more important to get high-quality software out the door quickly. In this digital age where software powers almost every part of our lives, businesses need to be quick to adapt and change in order to stay competitive. The software development business has gone through a huge paradigm shift to meet this need: Cloud-Based Continuous Integration and Continuous Deployment (CI/CD).

When you combine cloud computing with CI/CD, you enter a new era where software creation and deployment are not limited by the limitations of on-premises infrastructure. Instead, cloud-based CI/CD gives software teams a flexible, scalable, and low-cost way to speed up and automate the software development process. This book, "Cloud-Based CI/CD for Software Teams," tells you everything you need to know to get around in this interesting area.

### Why CI/CD is Important for 21st Century Software Development

Before we go into more detail about cloud-based CI/CD, it's important to know how important CI/CD is in current software development.

### How Fast Things Are Changing

These days, software is what makes new things possible. Software drives growth in everything from mobile apps and e-commerce sites to healthcare systems and self-driving cars. There are, however, some problems that come with this fast growth. Users almost always expect software to be updated with new features and bug fixes. Software updates once a year or twice a year are becoming less common.

### Meeting the Needs of Users

People are used to tech giants like Amazon, Google, and Apple giving them smooth, feature-packed encounters. In terms of speed and responsiveness, they expect all software companies to be the same. Companies need to be able to offer software updates quickly and without causing too many problems for users to stay interested and happy.

### Making sure of quality

Quality should always come first, though, not speed. There needs to be a lot of software that is stable and works well. Bugs and other problems are more likely to appear when changes are done often. To make sure that changes to software don't hurt the user experience, this needs strict testing and quality assurance measures.

### An edge over the competition

In a crowded market where new ideas are always being made, being able to quickly add new features and changes can give you an edge. Companies that can quickly adapt to changes in the market are more likely to gain market share and stay ahead of the competition in their fields.

### The Start of CI/CD

Continuous Integration (CI) and Continuous Deployment (CD) were created to deal with the problems that come up in modern software development, which is fast-paced, careful about quality, and very competitive.

### Integration that never stops (CI)

CI is the process of immediately adding changes to a shared repository made by multiple contributors, followed by automated build and testing. The main goal is to find problems with integration as early as possible in the creation process. CI makes it easier for people to work together, reduces code issues, and makes sure that the software is always ready to be deployed.

### Deployment that never stops (CD)

CD adds to the CI process so that changes to code can be automatically pushed to production or staging environments. CD tries to get rid of all manual work in the release process. This lowers the chance of mistakes and makes sure that end users always have access to the most up-to-date code. To keep applications stable, CD pipelines often include testing, tracking, and rollback features.

### Problems with Putting CI/CD into Action

CI/CD has a lot of potential benefits, but it can be hard to put into practice, especially in big, complicated organizations. There are some problems that need to be fixed before CI/CD can reach its full potential.

### Limitations on Infrastructure

CI/CD pipelines may need a lot of resources and may not be able to be supported by traditional on-premises systems. This can cause problems and hold up the growth process.

### Complexity of the toolchain

A lot of different tools are used in CI/CD processes, such as version control systems, build servers, testing frameworks, and tools for orchestrating deployments. It can be hard to make these tools work together smoothly.

### Changes in Culture

There is more to CI/CD than just technology. It's also about attitude and how things are done. Teams need to adopt a DevOps approach that stresses working together, talking to each other, and automating tasks. For some companies, this may mean changing the way they do things.

### Safety and Following the Rules

If they are not handled properly, automated pipelines can pose security risks. During the CI/CD process, it is very important to keep code, dependencies, and private data safe.

### What the Cloud Does for CI/CD

This is where the cloud comes in handy. The way businesses handle their IT infrastructure has changed a lot because of cloud computing. The cloud fits perfectly with the ideas of CI/CD because it offers resources on demand, can be scaled up or down, and is flexible.

### How to Scale

The option to change the size of resources as needed is one of the best things about the cloud. This flexibility is very helpful for CI/CD processes because it lets teams run tests at the same time, handle demand spikes, and make the best use of resources.

### Being flexible

Many services and tools are available from cloud companies, which lets businesses make their CI/CD pipelines fit their needs. There are many ways to improve CI/CD workflows in the cloud, such as using Kubernetes to handle containers, AWS Lambda for serverless computing, or managed databases.

### Low-cost performance

It can also be cheap to use CI/CD in the cloud. With pay-as-you-go pricing plans, businesses don't have to pay for infrastructure up front, which saves them money. Cloud service companies also provide cost management tools that help businesses keep track of their spending and make the most of it.

### World Reach

There are data centers and areas for cloud service providers all over the world. Companies with a global footprint can put software in use closer to the people who will be using it, which lowers latency and makes the user experience better.

### The Rise of CI/CD in the Cloud

Cloud-Based CI/CD is a powerful method that uses cloud resources to automate and speed up software creation and deployment. It was created when CI/CD and cloud computing came together. This book will show you how to use this powerful combination to your advantage.

Why use CI/CD in the cloud?

**Scalability:** The cloud gives companies almost endless resources, so they can run large test suites and send software to people all over the world without worrying about infrastructure.

**Flexibility:** Cloud companies provide a wide range of CI/CD services and tools to meet different needs. Machine learning services and tasks that don't need a server are all in the cloud.

**Cost Optimization:** The cloud lets businesses make the best use of their resources and use cost management tools to keep their CI/CD costs in check.

**Global Deployment:** With cloud-based CI/CD, companies can put their software in more than one area, making it more available and lowering latency for users all over the world.

What This Book Will Teach You

**Fundamentals of CI/CD:** To begin, we'll put the groundwork and make sure you have a solid grasp of the CI/CD principles, practices, and terms.

**Cloud Infrastructure for CI/CD:** You will learn how to pick the best cloud provider, set up CI/CD settings, and keep costs low.

**CI/CD Pipelines Designing in the Cloud:** We'll get down to the specifics of how to make CI/CD pipelines work well in the cloud, focusing on best practices and Infrastructure as Code (IaC) concepts.

**Automated Testing in CI/CD:** Quality assurance is very important, and we'll talk about the different kinds of automated testing, how they can be used in CI/CD processes, and ways to make sure the quality of software.

For continuous integration in the cloud, this part will go over how to set up CI environments, start builds and tests, handle build artifacts, and think about CI/CD security.

**Continuous Deployment in the Cloud:** Now we'll move on to the CD phase. Here, you will learn how to set up CD environments, schedule deployments, and make sure your apps are stable and reliable.

**Advanced CI/CD Topics:** We'll talk about advanced CI/CD topics like blue/green deployments, canary releases, containerization, orchestration, scalability, and speed optimization for people who want to get better at it.

**Security in Cloud-Based CI/CD:** Security is very important, and we'll show you how to deal with security issues in CI/CD pipelines, such as scans, compliance, governance, managing secrets, and controlling access.

**Real-life Case Studies:** We'll use real-life examples to show how companies of all sizes and in all kinds of businesses have used cloud-based CI/CD successfully. These case studies show what can be done in the real world and what can be learned from experience.

**Best Practices and Tips:** The book is full of best practices, tips, and strategies that were put together by people who have worked in the field for a long time. We'll point out common mistakes you should avoid and give you tips on how to keep getting better.

**What's Next for CI/CD in the Cloud:** Because technology is always changing, we'll also talk about new trends and tools that will affect cloud-based CI/CD.

### People who should read this book

The book "Cloud-Based CI/CD for Software Teams" is written for many people, from business leaders and software workers to DevOps engineers and IT managers. This book shows you how to learn cloud-based CI/CD and take your software development to a whole new level, no matter if you work for a startup, a large company, or an open-source project.

**Developers:** Learn how to automate and streamline your development processes so that your code is always being checked, deployed, and integrated.

For DevOps Engineers, learn about the best ways to manage CI/CD processes in the cloud, make the best use of resources, and keep your deployments safe.

IT managers, learn how cloud-based CI/CD can speed up the delivery of software, cut costs, and make your development teams more productive overall.

**Leaders in business:** Learn how cloud-based CI/CD can help your business in terms of speed, quality, and being competitive in the market. Find out how CI/CD can help you come up with new ideas and make customers happy.

### The Road Ahead

As we start our journey through the world of Cloud-Based CI/CD, I want you to be interested and excited about each part. These pages have something useful for everyone, whether you are new to CI/CD or have been doing it for a long time. Software development changes so quickly that it's hard to keep up. This book will teach you the tools and methods you need to stay on top of this exciting field.

Let's dive in and see what Cloud-Based CI/CD can do for us. This will give your software teams the tools they need to make software creation and delivery even better.

## 1. Definition of Cloud-Based CI/CD

CI/CD, which stands for Continuous Integration and Continuous Deployment, are now necessary ways to make software today. By using these methods together, called CI/CD, software teams can make the process of making, testing, and deploying apps faster and easier. Adding cloud computing to CI/CD, on the other hand, has created a new way of doing things called "Cloud-Based CI/CD." This piece will explain what Cloud-Based CI/CD is, why it's important, and how it's changing the way software is delivered in the cloud.

How to Understand CI/CD

Before we get into the details of Cloud-Based CI/CD, let's talk about what Continuous Integration (CI) and Continuous Deployment (CD) really mean.

Integration that never stops (CI)

Multiple writers' changes to code are automatically added to a shared repository several times a day as part of a development process called "continuous integration." The main goal is to find and fix integration problems as early as possible in the creation process. CI processes usually have steps like static code analysis, unit testing, and compiling the code.

Deployment that never stops (CD)

Continuous Deployment is an add-on to CI that makes it easy to push changes to code to production or testing environments as soon as they pass all tests. CD makes sure that changes to the code are directly available to end users with little to no work on their part. Integration testing, user acceptance testing, and performance testing are some of the other steps that are often added to CD pipelines to make sure that the software that is released is stable and reliable.

Introducing CI/CD in the cloud

Cloud-Based CI/CD means adding cloud computer services to the CI/CD process. It uses cloud tools, platforms, and services to make the whole process of delivering software better and more efficient. The way this method works is a big step forward for CI/CD because it uses cloud providers' scalability, flexibility, and low costs to their fullest.

Important Parts of CI/CD in the Cloud

**Cloud Infrastructure:** Amazon Web Services (AWS), Microsoft Azure, Google Cloud Platform (GCP), and other cloud providers host and handle infrastructure resources for cloud-based CI/CD. Virtual machines, containers, databases, and networking parts are some of these tools.

**Containerization:** In Cloud-Based CI/CD, containers like Docker containers are often used. Theygive you a standard way to package apps and the libraries they need, so you can use them in any context without any problems.

**Serverless Computing:** Platforms that don't run servers, like AWS Lambda and Azure Functions, let you run code without having to handle servers. Serverless is often used in CI/CD pipelines to run specific tasks or microservices.

**Orchestration:** Kubernetes and other orchestration tools are often used in cloud-based CI/CD workflows to manage containerized services and apps. Assuring efficient resource distribution, load balancing, and scalability is what orchestration does.

**handled Services:** Some parts of the CI/CD pipeline can be handled by cloud providers. Some of these services are databases, message queues, and tracking tools that make things easier for development teams.

Why cloud-based CI/CD is better

1. **Ability to grow**
   It's easy to scale up or down cloud services based on demand. This ability to grow is especially helpful when testing, launching apps, or dealing with traffic spikes. Teams no longer have to set up and run on-premises infrastructure to handle different amounts of work.
2. **Using resources well**
   You only pay for the tools you use when they are in the cloud. With this pay-as-you-go strategy, you don't have to buy hardware up front, and teams can make the best use of their resources, which saves money.
3. **Being flexible**
   Cloud service companies provide a wide range of tools and services that can be customized to meet the needs of CI/CD pipelines. The cloud gives you a lot of choices, like using machine learning services for testing or serverless features for automating tasks.
4. **Around the world**
   Cloud service providers run data centers and regions all over the world. This lets businesses put their software in places near to where people use it. This global reach cuts down on delay and makes the experience better for customers all over the world.
5. **Automated**

Cloud-based CI/CD makes it possible to automate the whole process of delivering software. Code changes move through the pipeline with little to no manual work because deployments, testing, and tracking are all done automatically.

Putting in place cloud-based CI/CD

1. **Picking a Cloud Provider:** Pick a cloud provider that fits the goals, budget, and technologies that your company already has. Some well-known cloud service companies are AWS, Azure, GCP, and others.
2. **Setting up environments for CI/CD:** Set up cloud environments that work with your CI/CD workflow. This includes setting up virtual machines, containers, and other tools that are needed.
3. **Adding CI/CD tools:** Add CI/CD tools like Jenkins, Travis CI, CircleCI, or cloud-native CI/CD services from the cloud source you chose.
4. **Automation:** Set up your CI/CD pipeline with steps for building, testing, and deploying code changes, and then automate it. To set up and run your process, use scripting or Infrastructure as Code (IaC).
5. **Testing and Quality Assurance:** Use automated testing methods, such as unit tests, integration tests, and end-to-end tests, to make sure the quality of the software is maintained all the way through the process.
6. **Security and Compliance:** Make sure that the CI/CD pipeline has security checks and compliance methods in place at all stages to protect code and infrastructure.
7. **Monitoring and Observability:** Use monitoring and observability tools to learn more about how well your system is working, how healthy your applications are, and how your users are feeling.
8. **Cost Management:** Use the tools that your cloud provider gives you to keep an eye on and handle costs well, making the best use of resources and allocating them wisely.

The world of software creation has changed a lot since cloud-based CI/CD came out. By using cloud resources, businesses can speed up the delivery of software, make better use of their resources, and improve the quality and dependability of their apps as a whole. It is easy to use, flexible, and cheap in the cloud, which fits perfectly with the goals of CI/CD and makes it a great tool for modern software teams.

Cloud-Based CI/CD is likely to become more popular as more businesses adopt cloud-based tools and methods. Teams that make software will be able to deliver software faster, more reliably, and with more flexibility to meet the changing needs of the digital world if they adopt this transformative method.

B. Importance of CI/CD in Modern Software Development

Continuous Integration and Continuous Deployment (CI/CD) have become important ways to make sure that software delivery is quick, reliable, and efficient in today's fast-paced world of software development. CI/CD is a big change in how software is built, tested, and released, and it has a lot of benefits for development teams and businesses. We will talk about how important CI/CD is in modern software development and how it affects quality, productivity, and user satisfaction.

1. Faster time to market and easy changes
   One of the best things about CI/CD is that it can speed up the software development process. Release cycles for traditional development methods are often long, with months or even years going by between big updates. If things move too slowly, you might miss out on market chances and become less competitive.
   CI/CD, on the other hand, encourages quick changes and lots of updates. Several times a day, developers can push changes to code to a common repository. These changes are fully tested by automated build and test pipelines, which lowers the chance of adding bugs. So, companies can give users new features, bug fixes, and other changes a lot faster, which shortens the time it takes to get a product to market.
2. Better code quality and dependability
   At every step of the production process, CI/CD stresses the importance of automated testing. This means that any changes to the code are always being tested with unit tests, integration tests, and even speed tests. Problems or regressions are found early on in the development process and fixed.
   This focus on testing makes the code better and more reliable. When developers know that their code has passed a lot of tests and won't cause any problems when it's put into use, they have more faith in it. This makes software more stable and less likely to crash or fail, which improves the user experience and lowers the cost of support and upkeep.
3. Working together and being open
   Continuous Integration and Continuous Delivery (CI/CD) makes the development process clear and pushes teams to work together. It's easier for team members to see what their coworkers are working on when changes to the code are constantly pushed out and merged. This encourages developers to work together by letting them look over each other's code, give comments, and share what they know.
   CI/CD pipelines also often make thorough logs and reports that

make it easier to see how a project is going and find any problems or bottlenecks. This opens up the development process so that project managers and other important people can make smarter choices about how to use resources and plan the project.

4. Ability to lower risk and roll back

There are always risks when making software. When software is put into work environments, problems can happen that were not expected, even if it was tested thoroughly. These risks are lessened by CI/CD, which automates the release process and lets you quickly go back to an earlier version.

Each change in a CI/CD process is first sent to a staging environment. This lets testing be done thoroughly in a setting that is similar to production. If problems are found, the release can be stopped and the bad version can be rolled back so that end users are not affected. This rollback feature lowers the chance of data loss and downtime, which is very important for high-availability apps.

5. Efficiency and the ability to grow

As software projects get more complicated, it gets harder to manage the development and release processes by hand. CI/CD tools and methods are very efficient and flexible, which makes it easier to work with big and complicated codebases.

Automation frees up time and effort for development and operations teams by doing jobs that need to be done over and over again and are prone to mistakes. This speed saves money because it helps companies better use their resources and get the most out of the time and skills of their development teams.

6. How Happy and Informed Your Customers Are

In the world of current software, making customers happy is very important. Users expect software to be updated and made better all the time to meet their changing wants. Companies can meet these expectations with CI/CD because it lets them quickly respond to user comments and release new features or bug fixes.

Developers can get feedback from users and make changes to the software based on that feedback by making small changes all the time. This iterative method makes sure that software stays in line with what users want and what the market needs. Because of this, businesses can stay competitive in a market that changes quickly and keep their customers happy.

7. Security and following the rules

In a time of growing cybersecurity risks and rules, CI/CD is also very important for making sure software is safe and follows the rules. Integrating automated security scans and vulnerability reviews into CI/CD pipelines makes it possible to find and fix security problems quickly.

CI/CD techniques also help businesses meet compliance standards by leaving a record of changes and deployments that can be checked. When it comes to fields with strict rules, like healthcare, banking, and government, this is especially important.

C. Purpose and Scope of the Book

Why and what this book is about

The Beginning

What the book is about and how big it is are basic ideas that both the author and the reader use to shape their work. In this sense, "Unveiling the Universe: Exploring the Cosmos from Earth and Beyond" is a thorough look into the universe and our place in it. This book explores the secrets of space, astronomy, and our quest to learn more about the universe in order to make you feel amazed, curious, and like you know more about it.

What the Book Is for

1. Teach and inform
   Making sure readers have a good understanding of astronomy and space exploration is one of the main goals of this book. It tries to explain difficult ideas in a way that is clear and interesting, so it can be read by people from a wide range of backgrounds, from people who are just interested in learning more to fans who want to dig deeper.
2. Make people wonder and be curious
   Cosmos has always been interesting to people, making them feel awe and wonder. This book shows the beauty, size, and complexity of the world in order to make you feel amazed again. Readers are urged to look at the universe with fresh eyes and an open mind by vivid descriptions, stunning images, and interesting stories.
3. Draw attention to the human quest for knowledge
   A big part of "Unveiling the Universe" is the past of how people have explored and found new things. It tells the story of how people have always wanted to learn more about the universe, from ancient civilizations that looked up at the stars to current space missions that explore faraway planets and galaxies. This history background shows how determined we are to understand the universe.
4. Help people learn about science
   In a time when knowing about science is more important than ever,

this book aims to help people learn more about it. By giving accurate information in an interesting way, it gives readers knowledge and critical thinking skills that go beyond the pages of the book, which leads to more informed conversations about the world.
5. Raise awareness about the environment

"Unveiling the Universe" is mostly about space and astronomy, but it also talks about how important Earth and its surroundings are in the bigger picture of the universe. It makes us realize how important it is to protect our planet and how fragile our survival is in the vastness of the universe.

What the Book Is About

1. What the Cosmos Means
   The first part of the book sets the scene by explaining the size of the universe, the past of people's interest in space, and the basic ideas behind astronomy and astrophysics. It looks at how telescopes and other astronomical tools have changed over time and how they have helped us understand the world.
2. The Sun and the Galaxy
   Readers go on a trip through the solar system, which is our own home in space. Asteroids, comets, planets, and moons of our solar system are all looked at in detail in this part, which goes from the hot sun to the faraway Kuiper Belt. The focus is on both what scientists know about these celestial objects and what they mean to people historically and culturally.
3. Stars and Events in the Stellar Field
   When the book talks about how stars are born, live, and die, it sheds light on the processes that power these huge objects in space. This book talks about the amazing things that happen with stars, like supernovae, black holes, and neutron stars. It also talks about how stars help make elements and galaxies.
4. The Milky Way and Other Galaxies
   The story takes readers on a trip through the Milky Way, which is our home galaxy, as well as other galaxies that are out there in the world. The structure of galaxies, the supermassive black holes at their cores, the expansion of the universe, and the search for life beyond Earth are some of the things that are talked about.
5. How people are exploring space
   This part talks about how people want to explore space beyond Earth's limits. It talks about the past of space travel, from the early

days of the space race to modern missions to the moon, Mars, and other places. Readers learn about the difficulties and successes of sending people into space and sending robots on tasks.
6. Mysteries and Unanswered Questions About the Universe
There are many references in the book to the fact that our knowledge of the universe is not full. This part talks about some of the biggest puzzles in cosmology, like what dark matter and dark energy are and how they work. It also talks about the Big Bang theory and the idea that there might be other universes out there.
7. "The Fragile Oasis": Green and Earth Awareness

Even though "Unveiling the Universe" is mostly about the universe, it also stresses how important Earth is in that setting. In light of what we know about the world, it talks about how important it is to care about the environment, be sustainable, and take care of our planet responsibly.

The book "Unveiling the Universe: Exploring the Cosmos from Earth and Beyond" is meant to teach, excite, and take readers on an exciting trip through the universe. The goal is to help people learn more about science, develop a deeper knowledge of the universe, and feel amazed and curious about it. In the fields of astronomy, cosmology, and space exploration, the book covers a lot of different themes. This gives readers a full picture of where we fit in the universe. In the end, this book encourages readers to take an intellectual and artistic trip to discover the universe's mysteries and our never-ending search for knowledge.

D. Target Audience

When you're writing information or talking to people, knowing who you're writing for is very important. Customers are very important when you're making a marketing campaign, writing a book, creating a website, or making a product. They shape your content and how well it works. This piece goes into detail about the idea of a target audience, how important it is to correctly identify them, and how to make content that will appeal to different groups of your audience.

Choosing the Right Audience

A statement, product, or service is meant to reach and interact with a certain group of people or organizations. This is called the target audience. Your content or offerings are more likely to be well received by this group because they share certain behaviors, hobbies, and needs. Finding and understanding your target audience well is like hitting the target; it makes sure that your efforts go to the people who are most likely to benefit from and be interested in what you have to give.

How important it is to know who your target audience is

1. Being relevant and customizing
   When you know who you're writing for, you can make content and experiences that are very important and unique. This makes it more likely that people will connect with your message because it goes directly to their wants, needs, and interests. A personalized method helps you and your audience feel like you know them and trust you.
2. Resource Allocation That Works
   Figuring out who your target group is helps you use your resources more wisely. When it comes to your marketing budget, time, or creative energy, focusing on the parts of your audience that are most likely to convert or engage will help you get the most out of your efforts and waste the least.
3. More participation and better communication
   Customizing your material to the people you want to reach improves communication and engagement. When your message speaks to the specific worries and hopes of your audience, it gets their attention and makes them want to act. In this case, it could mean more people visiting your website, more clicks, or a higher percentage of sales.
4. Better development of products
   Businesses need to know who their target customer is in order to make good products. Knowing your audience's problems, wants, and tastes will help you make goods and services that meet their needs better. This not only makes the goods more likely to succeed, but it also makes customers more loyal.
5. Getting used to changes in the market

The market is always changing, and people's tastes can shift quickly. You can better deal with these changes if you have a deep understanding of your target group. If you pay attention to changes in your audience's habits and expectations, you can adapt your tactics and products to stay relevant and competitive.

Different Kinds of Audiences

1. Grouping people by demographics
   Demographic segmentation divides the target audience into groups based on things like age, gender, wealth, level of education, marital status, and where they live. For instance, a makeup brand might aim for young women in cities who make a certain amount of money.
2. Grouping people by psychographics
   When you use psychographic segmentation, you look at the audi-

ence's mental and social traits. This covers things like values, interests, hobbies, and personality traits. An outdoor adventure company might try to attract thrill-seekers who value events over things.

3. Separating people by behavior
   Behavioral segmentation looks at how the viewer acts and behaves. It looks at things like past purchases, company loyalty, usage patterns, and how people react to marketing messages. A fitness app might try to get people who have been working out regularly in the past.
4. Grouping by technology
   In this digital age, technological division is very important. It includes putting people into groups based on how they use and adopt technology. One example is a software company that might go after companies that use cloud-based services.
5. B2B and B2C People
   You can also divide audiences into groups based on whether they are businesses (B2B) or individual customers (B2C). Each type of group has different wants, needs, and ways of making decisions and buying things.
6. Very specific and niche audiences

Some businesses and content makers focus on niche or specialized groups of people who have very specific wants or needs. This could include groups of people who share a hobby, academic researchers, or fans of certain areas.

Figuring out who you want to reach

1. Studying the market
   Do in-depth market study to learn more about the people who might be interested in your product. This can include things like behavioral trends, psychographic insights, and demographic information. To get a better idea, you can use market reports, polls, and data analytics.
2. Making profiles of customers
   Make detailed profiles of customers or "personas" that reflect different groups of your audience. Age, gender, hobbies, problems, and goals should all be written down in these personas. It's easier to make your content fit your viewers when you can picture them in this way.

3. A look at the competition
   Look at what your rivals are doing to see who they are trying to reach and how they are doing it. If you know what your competitors are doing, you can find gaps or chances in the market.
4. Talking and getting feedback
   If you can, interact with the people who are already following you. Get feedback from people by using polls, social media, or customer reviews. Listen to what they have to say, what hurts them, and what they want.
5. Testing and making changes

When you start to interact with your target group, be ready to test your ideas and change how you do things. Sometimes, you may need to add to what you thought you knew about your audience based on facts and interactions from the real world.

Changing content to fit different groups of people

1. Use the Right Tone and Language
   Your audience's tastes should guide the language and tone of what you write. For instance, content for a younger audience might use casual language and a conversational tone, while content for a professional audience might need to be written in a more formal and scientific way.
2. Deal with certain points of pain
   Figure out what your audience is having trouble with and what hurts them, and then add that to your material. Give them answers, ideas, or direction that are directly related to what they need.
3. Draw attention to important benefits
   Make it clear to your audience what benefits your product, service, or message are most important to them. Show them how it makes their lives better, fixes their problems, or gives them what they want.
4. Appeal to the eye
   Think about how your public likes to see things. Use graphics, images, and design features that speak to them. The way your information looks can have a big effect on how people react to it.
5. Make layouts fit the content
   There may be different types of people in your group who like different types of content. Some people might like videos more than written pieces or podcasts. Provide information in different formats to meet the needs of a wide range of people.

6. Being consistent and real
   Make sure that your brand and messages are the same on all sites and interactions. Authenticity is very important. Make sure that the values of your business and your audience are reflected in your content.
7. Test and improve

Always keep an eye on how your content is doing and be ready to make changes. A/B testing can help you figure out which versions of your content work best with different groups of people.

Knowing your audience is one of the most important parts of communicating and writing material that gets results. Knowing what your audience likes, needs, and how they like to be influenced can help you make your content more interesting to them. It doesn't matter if you're a business trying to connect with customers or a writer trying to connect with readers—addressing the unique aspects of your target group is a powerful way to succeed. There is a lot of information out there, so what makes you stand out and get people to engage with you is how deeply you connect with them.

E. Overview of the Book's Structure

Before getting into a book, readers often look for a map to help them find their way around. This is where the framework of the book becomes very important. A good organization not only arranges the information in a way that makes sense, but it also helps the reader understand and be interested in what they are reading. This article will give you a full picture of how our book, "Architecting Knowledge: Navigating the Landscape of Information," is put together. The goal of the book is to look into the details of knowledge management and information architecture, as well as their important part in the digital age.

The Beginning of the Book

Before we get into how the book is put together, let's take a quick look at its main idea and goal.

"Architecting Knowledge" is a book that tries to explain how to organize and manage knowledge in the digital age. Knowledge management and information design have never been more important than they are now, when the world is full of data and information. For professionals, academics, and enthusiasts interested in comprehending the ideas, methods, and challenges of managing and architecting knowledge, this book aims to provide a thorough guide.

How the book is put together

There are different parts to the book, and each one talks about a different area of knowledge management and information architecture. According to the structure, readers will be taken on a logical trip from basic ideas to more advanced strategies. This will help them fully grasp the topic.

1. The Basics of Knowledge Management
   This first part sets the scene by explaining the basic ideas behind information management. It's a good starting point for people who are new to the subject or want to review the basics.
   Chapter 1: An Overview of Knowledge Management
   Gives an outline of knowledge management, how it has changed over time, and what it means in today's world.
   Describes important terms and ideas, like clear knowledge, tacit knowledge, and knowledge sharing.
   Chapter 2: The Lifecycle of Knowledge Management
   The stages of the knowledge management process are looked at, such as creating knowledge, capturing it, storing it, sharing it, and using it.
   Talks about how organizational culture and technology play a part in each step.
   Chapter 3: Taxonomies and Knowledge Maps
   It talks about how to use knowledge mapping and how categories were made.
   Describes how important it is to organize information so that it can be easily found and used.
2. The Basics of Information Architecture

This part moves from talking about knowledge management in a wider sense to talking about information architecture in more detail. It gives you the tools you need to understand how information is stored and viewed efficiently.
   Chapter 4: An Introduction to IT Architecture
   Explains what information design is and why it's important in digital settings.
   It talks about how information design and user experience are connected.
   Chapter 5: Sorting cards and user research
   Looks at approaches to information architecture that focus on the user, such as card sorting and
      user studies.

Describes how empathy can be used to create information systems that meet the needs of users.

**Chapter 6 is about designing taxonomies and navigation systems.**

Explores the ins and outs of taxonomy design, covering both hierarchy and faceted taxonomies.

Talks about navigation devices and how they help people find information easily.

**Part 3: Advanced Strategies for Managing Knowledge**

This part goes over more advanced knowledge management strategies and techniques, building on what you learned in the earlier sections.

**Chapter 7: Groups of people who work together**

looks at the idea of communities of practice as a powerful way to share information.

Talks about how technology and social networks can help build communities of practice.

**Chapter 8: Holding on to and sharing knowledge**

Deals with the challenges that come up when organizations try to keep and share information.

Looks at ways to keep institutional knowledge alive and give it to future generations.

Artificial intelligence and knowledge management are covered in Chapter 9.

looks into how artificial intelligence (AI) and information management can work together.

Looks at how AI technologies can improve finding information, suggesting content, and helping people make decisions.

**Section 4: New Trends and the Big Picture**

Looking ahead, the last part of the book talks about new trends and what the future holds for knowledge management and information design.

**Chapter 10: Privacy and Moral Issues with Data**

This article talks about the moral aspects of knowledge management, mainly when it comes to data privacy and information security.

Talks about what groups need to do to keep sensitive information safe.

**Chapter 11: What's Next for Knowledge Management**

Thinks about how trends like blockchain, augmented reality, and the Internet of Things (IoT) might affect the future of information management.

Talks about how knowledge managers' jobs are changing in a digital world that is always changing.

**Chapter 12: The End and What to Do Next**

Describes the most important ideas from the book.

It encourages people to use the ideas and methods of information architecture and knowledge management in their personal and work lives.

The book "Architecting Knowledge: Navigating the Landscape of Information" is a well-organized and thorough look at information architecture and knowledge management. It is divided into clear parts and chapters that take readers from basic ideas to more complex strategies, all while keeping new trends and ethical issues in mind. By following this well-thought-out plan, readers can really understand how to use information to your advantage in this modern era. This book's structure makes sure that you get a full picture of the topic and are ready to handle the complicated worlds of knowledge management and information architecture, whether you are a knowledge management professional, a student, or someone who is just interested in how information is changing.

# Chapter 1

## Fundamentals of CI/CD

CI/CD, which stands for Continuous Integration and Continuous Deployment, has changed the way software is built, tested, and released. These methods have become necessary for modern software development because they help teams make high-quality software quickly and easily. We'll talk about the basics of CI/CD in this guide, including its principles, benefits, key practices, and the tools that are usually used in CI/CD workflows.

### A Quick Look at CI/CD

### What does CI/CD mean?

CI/CD, which stands for "Continuous Integration and Continuous Deployment," are techniques that make the process of making software easier. They involve automating different parts of creation, testing, and deployment so that software can be sent out more often and more reliably.

### How software development has changed over time

Creating software used to be a slow and laborious process that had to be done by hand. Developers would work on separate pieces of code, and when they were combined with code from other team members, it often caused problems and disagreements. Testing and release were usually done by hand, which took a lot of time and could go wrong.

### Why CI/CD Is Important

As technology changed and software became more important to businesses, there was a need for a faster and more reliable way to make and send software. The introduction of automation, continuous integration of code changes, and continuous deployment to production environments were introduced by CI/CD to handle these challenges.

### The basics of CI/CD

### Automating Things

CI/CD is based on automating things. It uses scripts and tools to do things like code integration, testing, and release without the developer having to do anything. By automating tasks, mistakes are less likely to happen, work is done faster, and standards are met.

### Integration That Never Stops

Continuous Integration means putting changes to code made by multiple workers into a shared repository on a regular basis and automatically. This process encourages cooperation and helps find integration problems early on.

### Deploying all the time

Continuous Deployment goes one step further than CI by putting changes to code into production environments automatically once all tests pass. This method makes sure that users get new features and bug fixes quickly.

### Testing All the Time

Unit tests, integration tests, and end-to-end tests are all types of testing that are automated as part of continuous testing. It makes sure that changes to the code are tested carefully at every stage of development, which lowers the chance of bugs.

### Change Control

Version control means keeping track of changes to code, working with other people, and keeping a log of changes to code using tools like Git. It lets workers work on different features or bug fixes at the same time without having to wait for each other.

### Checking and Giving Feedback

Data from production settings is collected as part of continuous monitoring and feedback. This information is used to learn more about how well an app works, how users act, and possible problems. Feedback loops help teams make choices based on data and make the quality of software better.

### Pros and cons of CI/CD

### Shorter time between development cycles

By automating human tasks, CI/CD shortens the time it takes to make software. Changes to the code can be quickly integrated, tested, and deployed by developers, which speeds up the delivery of new features.

### Better quality software

With automated testing and continuous merging, problems and bugs are found early on in the development process. This improves the quality of the software and lowers the amount of bugs that get into production.

### Less work done by hand

CI/CD pipelines automate jobs that used to be done by hand, like integrating code and deploying it. This cuts down on the work that needs to be done by hand, giving developers more time to work on unique, important tasks.

### More working together

CI/CD makes it easier for the management, testing, and development teams to work together. Multiple developers can work at the same time, and changes are made automatically through processes.

### Better security

CI/CD pipelines can have security checks added that look through code for bugs and compliance problems. Concerns about security are dealt with ahead of time, which lowers the chance of security leaks.

### Time to Market Faster

CI/CD speeds up development cycles and automates tasks so that organizations can give people new features and updates more quickly. This shorter time to market can give you an edge over your competitors.

## Parts of the CI/CD Pipeline

### Place to store source code

A source code repository is a place where coders can store and organize their code. Git is a well-known version control system that can be used for this.

### Set up automation

As part of build automation, the source code is compiled into files that can be run. This step checks the code to make sure it is right and can be run.

### Testing by Machine

Unit tests, integration tests, and other types of tests that make sure the code works and is right are all part of automated testing.

### The Artifact Repository

The code files that have been compiled and tested are kept in an artifact repository. This makes them available for deployment.

### Automation of deployment

Changing code in different settings, like development, testing, staging, and production, is what deployment automation is all about. Automation keeps things consistent and cuts down on distribution mistakes.

### Checking and Giving Feedback

Monitoring production settings all the time gives useful information about how applications work and how users act. This information helps make choices about future development and finds problems quickly so they can be fixed.

## Key Things to Do in CI/CD

Git keeps track of changes.

Git is the normal way to keep track of versions in CI/CD. It makes it easy for developers to work together, keep track of changes, and handle code repositories.

### Testing by Computer

A key part of CI/CD is automated testing. Unit tests, integration tests, and end-to-end tests all make sure that changes to the code are fully checked out.

### Use of Docker for containerization

Docker containers make it possible for apps to run in a consistent and portable environment. A lot of the time, containers are used to package apps and the libraries they need.

### Putting together things with Kubernetes

Kubernetes is a powerful platform for orchestrating containers that makes it easy to launch, scale, and manage containerized apps.

### It stands for Infrastructure as Code.

In IaC, infrastructure is defined using code, which makes it possible for infrastructure tools to be automatically set up and managed.

### Strategies for Deployment

Blue-green deployment and canary releases are two deployment methods that help companies make code changes with little risk and downtime.

### Feedback and monitoring all the time

Monitoring production settings all the time gives you real-time information about how applications are running and how users are behaving. Teams can make changes based on data when they use feedback loops.

### Tech and Tools for CI/CD

CI/CD pipelines often use a number of tools and technologies to automate different jobs and processes. These are some well-known ones:

### John Jenkins

Jenkins is an open-source automation service that makes it easier to test, build, and release changes to code. A lot of plugins and connections can be used with it.

### CI Travis

The continuous development service Travis CI runs in the cloud and tests and deploys code automatically. The format works well for GitHub projects.

### CI Circle

CircleCI is another CI/CD platform in the cloud that lets you test and release software projects automatically.

### Use GitLab CI/CD

GitLab has CI/CD features built right into its platform, which makes setting up CI/CD workflows easy for GitLab users.

A docker

Docker is a tool for containerization that makes it easier to package apps and their dependencies into containers that can be easily deployed.

To Kubernetes

Kubernetes is a platform for orchestrating containers that makes it easy to run and grow containerized apps.

Change the terrain

A well-known Infrastructure as Code (IaC) tool called Terraform lets developers use code to describe and set up infrastructure resources.

The god Prometheus

Prometheus is an open-source tracking and alerting toolkit that is often used in CI/CD pipelines for continuous monitoring.

Continuous Integration and Continuous Deployment (CI/CD) are big changes in how software is made, checked, and put into use. By following the ideas of automation, continuous integration, continuous release, and other similar ideas, businesses can speed up the development process, make software better, and work together better.

We've talked about the basics of CI/CD in this guide, from its ideas and advantages to important methods and popular tools. CI/CD is now an important part of modern software development because it helps companies meet the needs of fast software release in the digital age. Understanding and using CI/CD practices can greatly improve your ability to create high-quality software quickly and reliably, no matter if you're a developer, a DevOps engineer, or the leader of a software team.

1.1 What Is CI/CD?

Continuous Integration (CI) and Continuous Deployment (CD) are two of the most important techniques used in current software development. They have changed how software is made, tested, and put into use, which has made software better and sped up release times. We will talk about the main ideas of CI/CD in this detailed guide. We will talk about what it is, how it works, its perks, and its part in the software development lifecycle.

What CI/CD Means

Integration that never stops (CI)

CI is a way of developing that focuses on adding changes to code to a shared repository instantly and on a regular basis. Developers merge their changes to the code into a central version control system, like Git, several times a day. CI is meant to find problems with integration early on in the creation process.

Some important CI ideas are:

Automatic Builds: When code changes, automatic builds happen to make sure that the software can be correctly compiled and packaged.

**Automated Testing:** Unit tests, integration tests, and sometimes end-to-end tests are run automatically to make sure that the changes to the code haven't caused any bugs.

**Frequent Integration:** Developers add changes to the code to the main file several times a day. This encourages teamwork and avoids "integration hell," which can happen when changes pile up over time.

**Version Control:** Changes to code are tracked by version control systems like Git. This lets writers work on different features or bug fixes at the same time without any problems.

**Feedback Loop:** CI tells writers right away if there are any problems or mistakes in the changes they make to the code. This quick feedback process pushes developers to fix problems quickly.

Deployment that never stops (CD)

CD adds to CI by putting code changes into production or other target settings automatically after they pass all the tests. CD wants to make the process of releasing and deploying smooth and reliable.

Some important ideas in CD are:

**Automation:** Deployment methods are automated so that people don't have to do as much work by hand and make fewer mistakes.

**Consistency:** CD makes sure that the same steps are taken for each release. This keeps things consistent and lowers the risk of problems during deployment.

**Rollbacks:** If there are problems with deployment or in production, CD techniques usually include automatic ways to go back to a stable version.

**Release Pipelines:** CD pipelines list the steps and actions that need to be taken for a release to go smoothly, from testing and building to staging and production.

**Monitoring and Feedback:** Continuous monitoring of production settings is part of CD so that problems can be found after deployment. Feedback is used to help make things better.

CI/CD: How It Works

It is the job of developers to make changes to code and send them to a version control system like Git. The CI/CD pipeline starts when this step is taken.

**Automatic Build:** The CI/CD process starts by building the software on its own based on the changes to the code. This makes sure the code can be correctly built and packaged.

**Automated Testing:** After that, unit tests, integration tests, and any other tests that are needed are run automatically. The pipeline may stop and the coder is told if any tests fail.

**Moving to Staging:** If all tests pass, the changes to the code are moved to a staging or pre-production system. As nearly as possible, this environment is set up like the production environment.

**More Testing:** To make sure the code changes meet the quality standards, more testing may be done in the staging environment. This could include speed, load, and user acceptance testing.

When changes are made to code and they pass all tests in the staging environment, they are

immediately sent to the production environment. In this step, methods for lowering risk may be used, such as blue-green deployment or canary releases.

**Monitoring and Feedback:** The production setting is monitored continuously as soon as it is put into use. Metrics and logs are kept to find problems, slowdowns, or other strange behavior. This feedback loop helps make more changes and, if needed, go back and fix things.

Pros and cons of CI/CD

**Faster Development Cycles:** CI/CD pipelines automate a lot of jobs that used to be done by hand, so developers can make changes to code and deliver them more often. This means that development processes are shorter and new features are released more quickly.

**Better Software:** Regular integration and automated tests help find and fix problems early in the development process. Because of this, the quality of the program is much better, and there are fewer bugs in production.

**Less work to be done by hand:** CI/CD pipelines automate boring and error-prone jobs, so people don't have to do as much work by hand during development, testing, and deployment.

**Better Teamwork:** Regular integration and automated tests make it easier for developers to work together. Early detection of conflicts and merging problems makes the development process go more smoothly.

**Better security:** Security checks can be added to CI/CD systems to look for holes in code and make sure it meets security standards. Concerns about security are dealt with ahead of time.

**Faster Time-to-Market:** CI/CD speeds up development cycles and automates processes, so companies can give people new features and updates more quickly. This shorter time to market can give you an edge over your competitors.

CI/CD, which stands for Continuous Integration and Continuous Deployment, are basic techniques used in current software development. They support automating tasks, working together, and getting good software to people faster and more reliably. By knowing the main ideas behind CI/CD, like continuous integration and continuous deployment, businesses can improve the way they make software and stay competitive in the digital world that is changing so quickly these days. CI/CD can help you release software more quickly, reliably, and creatively, no matter if you're a developer, a DevOps engineer, or just involved in software development in some other way.

## 1.2 Benefits of CI/CD

Quality and speed are the most important things in the world of software creation. CI/CD, or Continuous Integration and Continuous Deployment, have become must-do tasks that provide many benefits. The methods used to create, test, and release software have changed a lot, making it possible for teams to quickly and accurately offer high-quality software. This complete guide will go into detail about the advantages of CI/CD, including how it speeds up development, raises the quality of software, encourages teamwork, protects data, and eventually leads to a shorter time to market.

Shorter time between development cycles

1. **Integration Often:** Continuous Integration (CI) pushes workers to add changes to a shared repository of code often. This keeps code from getting out of date and makes it easy to find and fix interface problems quickly.
2. **Automated Builds:** CI/CD pipelines make sure that changes to the code can be properly compiled and packaged by automating the build process. This means that coders don't have to build the software by hand, which saves a lot of time.
3. **Continuous Testing:** An important part of CI/CD is automated testing. It means constantly and continuously running different kinds of tests, such as unit tests, integration tests, and end-to-end tests. CI/CD cuts down on the time needed to fix bugs by finding them early in the development process.
4. **Quick Feedback:** CI/CD lets writers get feedback quickly. As soon as a change is made to the code, automated tests run and any problems are mentioned right away. This feedback loop helps writers fix problems quickly, so there are no delays.
5. **Shorter Development Cycles:** Integration that happens often, testing that is done automatically, and getting feedback quickly all work together to make development cycles much shorter. When developers work on adding new features or fixing bugs, they can be sure that their changes will be quickly added and tested.

Better quality software

1. **Automated Testing:** Every time the code changes, CI/CD processes run a set of automated tests, such as unit tests, integration tests, and end-to-end tests. This thorough testing method helps find and fix bugs early on in the development process, which lowers the number of problems that get to production.
2. CD pipelines make sure that the same rollout process is used for every release, which is called consistency. This makes it less likely that mistakes will happen during deployment or that settings will change between environments.
3. **Version Control:** CI/CD uses version control tools, such as Git, to keep track of changes to code. Version control keeps track of all the times that code has been changed so that writers can work on different features or bug fixes at the same time without running into problems.
4. **Constant Watching:** CD includes watching over work environments all the time. With this real-time tracking, teams can quickly find problems and fix them before they affect users. It also gives information about how well an app works and how users behave, which can be used to make more changes.
5. **backup Mechanisms:** CD pipelines often have automated backup mechanisms built in. If there are problems with the deployment or in production, the pipeline can automatically go back to a version that was safe before. This cuts down on downtime and the effect on users.

Better collaboration

1. **Integration Often:** Continuous Integration (CI) tells writers to add their changes to a shared repository several times a day. This regular integration makes it easier for people to work together by making sure that changes to the code are smoothly added and that problems are found early.
2. **Automated Testing:** CI/CD processes include automated testing, which gives a fair look at the quality of the code. Automated tests can help developers make sure that their changes to the code are correct and up to code standards.
3. **Code Reviews:** An important part of CI/CD is code reviews. As a way to give comments and make sure the quality of the code, developers look over each other's changes. This way of working together helps keep the quality of the code good.

4. **Cross-Functional Teams:** CI/CD pushes developers, testers, and operations professionals to work together on teams that do more than one thing. These groups work together to make sure that changes to the code not only work, but also are fast, safe, and effective.
5. **Communication:** CI/CD practices usually include clear ways for people to share problems, talk about changes to the code, and plan deployments. Open conversation makes it easier for people to work together and be honest.

Better security

1. **Automated Security Scans:** CI/CD pipelines can include static code analysis and vulnerability checking as part of automated security scans. These scans look for security holes in the code and let writers know about them early on.
2. **Compliance Checks:** CI/CD pipelines can make sure that changes to code are in line with security rules and standards by using compliance checks. This proactive method lowers the chance of security leaks.
3. **Consistent contexts:** Continuous integration (CI) makes sure that changes to code are applied the same way in all contexts. This consistency reduces the chance of security holes occurring because of differences in setup.
4. **Quick Action:** Since production settings are constantly watched, security problems or strange behavior can be found quickly. As soon as problems are found, teams can act quickly to lower security risks.
5. **Safe Deployment:** CD pipelines can use safe deployment methods, like encryption and authentication, to keep private data safe and make sure users can safely access apps.

Time to Market Faster

1. **Automation:** CI/CD takes care of a lot of chores that used to have to be done by hand during development, testing, and deployment. This technology cuts down on the time and work needed to make changes to software.
2. **Continuous Integration:** The code changes are always ready to be deployed because they are integrated often. Because of this, companies can share new features or bug fixes as soon as they are finished and tested.

3. **Deployment Strategies:** Code deployment techniques like blue-green deployment and canary releases make it possible for companies to make code changes with little risk and downtime. These methods make it possible for new features to be released quickly.
4. **Monitoring and Feedback:** Monitoring production settings all the time gives you real-time information about how applications are running and how users are behaving. This feedback helps organizations make more changes and deal with problems quickly.
5. **A competitive edge:** Companies that use CI/CD can release software changes and improvements more quickly than their rivals. In the market, this speed can give you a big edge over your competitors.When it comes to making software, Continuous Integration and Continuous Deployment (CI/CD) are very helpful in many ways. CI/CD techniques are essential to the success of modern software development because they speed up development cycles, improve software quality, make it easier for people to work together, make it safer, and get software to market faster.

Companies that use CI/CD can make their development processes more efficient, make their software more reliable, and better adapt to changing market needs. CI/CD practices can help your company and its users by making software delivery more efficient, reliable, and creative. This is true whether you're a developer, a DevOps engineer, or involved in software development in some other way.

1.3 Key Principles and Concepts

Important ideas and rules behind Continuous Integration and Continuous Deployment (CI/CD)

You can think of Continuous Integration and Continuous Deployment (CI/CD) as more than just methods. They are based on important ideas and ideals that make them work. We will talk about the main ideas and principles behind CI/CD in this detailed guide. These include automation, continuous integration, continuous deployment, version control, testing, and tracking.

**Automating Things**

1. **Builds that are done automatically:** CI/CD systems make it easy to compile source code, run tests, and package apps. This makes sure that changes to the code can be made consistently and without any help from a person.
2. **Automated Testing:** When the code changes, automated tests, such as unit tests, integration tests, and end-to-end tests, run themselves.

Automation makes sure that code is tested fully and that problems are found quickly.
3. **Deployment Automation:** Continuous Delivery (CD) techniques automate the deployment process, making sure that changes to the code are sent to all environments in the same way and without any extra steps that need to be done by hand.
4. **Infrastructure as Code (IaC):** defining infrastructure resources (like computers and databases) using code is an automation idea called Infrastructure as Code. This lets infrastructure be set up and managed automatically, making sure that everything is the same every time.
5. **Constant Watching and Response:** Production settings are constantly watched over by computers, which finds problems, mistakes, and strange behavior right away. Monitoring gives information that helps make things better and can set off automatic reactions to problems.

Integration that never stops (CI)

1. **Frequently Integrating:** Developers are told to add their changes to the public repository several times a day. This keeps code from getting old and lowers the chance of problems during integration.
2. **Automated Builds:** When changes are made to code and pushed to the repository, automated build steps start. This makes sure the code can be built, compiled, and packaged properly.
3. **Automated Testing:** As part of the CI process, automated tests, such as unit tests and integration tests, are run regularly. These tests make sure that changes to the code are right and work as expected.
4. **Version Control:** To keep track of changes to code, version control tools like Git are used. The CI method makes sure that changes are made without any problems when developers work on different branches.
5. **Quick Feedback:** CI gives developers quick feedback by running tests right away and sharing any problems. This feedback loop helps developers solve issues quickly, which keeps the quality of the code high.

Deployment that never stops (CD)

1. **Automated Deployment:** CD pipelines make sure that code changes are released without any interaction from a person. This technology lowers the chance of mistakes made by people.
2. **Strategies for Deployment:** Blue-green deployment and canary releases are two common strategies for deployment that are used in CD practices. With these methods, companies can make code changes with little risk and downtime.
3. **Mechanisms for rolling back:** If there are problems with production or during deployment, CD pipelines can immediately go back to a stable version that was made earlier. This keeps downtime to a minimum and keeps users from being affected badly.
4. **Staging settings:** CD pipelines often have staging settings that are very similar to production. Changes to the code are put into these settings before they are put into production. This lets more testing and validation happen.
5. **Continuous Monitoring:** An important part of CD is keeping an eye on work environments all the time. It includes getting real-time information about how well an app works, how users act, and errors. Monitoring helps find problems after deployment and leads to more changes.

Change Control

1. **Code History:** Version control tools keep track of changes to code over time. Developers can see when and why changes were made with this information. This makes it easier to find problems and fix them.
2. **Branches and Merges:** When developers make changes to code, they work on different branches. You can make branches for testing, adding new features, or fixing bugs. Integration is made easier by combining code from different branches into the main file.
3. **Resolving Conflicts:** Version control systems have tools for dealing with conflicts that happen when different coders make changes to the same code. Before code is merged, conflicts are found and fixed.
4. **Collaboration:** Version control systems let writers work together by letting them make changes to different pieces of code at the same time. It also makes code reviews and conversations about possible changes easier.
5. **Rolling back the code:** If there are problems or regressions in production, version control systems let you go back to a safe version of the code that was used before.

Checking out

1. **Unit Tests:** These tests look at single pieces of code, like functions or classes, to make sure they work right when run by themselves.
2. **Integration Tests:** These tests make sure that different parts or services of a program work together and interact with each other correctly.
3. **End-to-End Tests:** These tests pretend that a customer is using the app and making sure that the whole thing works right.
4. **Regression Tests:** These tests make sure that that current features still work after new code changes are made. They help keep problems from coming back after being fixed.
5. **Performance and Load Testing:** This type of testing checks how well an app works in different situations, like when it has a lot of users or a lot of data to process.
6. **Security Testing:** Static code analysis and vulnerability checking are two types of security testing that find and fix security holes in code.

People who will actually use the app are used in user acceptance testing (UAT) to make sure it meets their needs and expectations.

Feedback and monitoring all the time

1. **Monitoring in real time:** Monitoring tools get info from production environments in real time. Metrics on application speed, error rates, resource use, and user interactions are all in this data.
2. **Sending alerts:** Monitoring tools can send alerts if certain conditions are met or if there are strange patterns in the data. Alerts let teams know about problems that need to be fixed right away.
3. **Feedback Loops:** Monitoring data is used to help with development by suggesting ways to make things better and fixing bugs. This feedback loop makes sure that teams are always working to improve the quality and dependability of the app.
4. **Log Analysis:** Problems are fixed by looking at log data to show where mistakes are coming from and how users are interacting with the app.
5. **Performance Optimization:** Ongoing tracking shows places where performance can be improved, which helps teams find and fix problems before they happen.These two technologies, Continuous Integration and Continuous Deployment (CI/CD), are based on a set of basic ideas and principles that help companies speed up software development, make code better, and release more reliable software

more often. CI/CD techniques are built on automation, version control, testing, and feedback and monitoring that happen all the time. You need to understand and follow these rules in order to get the most out of CI/CD and be successful in current software development.

1.4 CI/CD Workflow Overview

Continuous Integration and Continuous Deployment (CI/CD) methods have changed the way software is made by automating and improving the whole process of delivering software. With these processes, companies can make, test, and release changes to code quickly and safely. This complete guide will give you a full picture of the CI/CD process, including its main steps, rules, and advantages.

How the CI/CD Workflow Works

1. Control of Versions

    Version control is the first step in the CI/CD process. This is a basic practice in software development. It is possible to keep track of changes to source code with version control tools like Git. When developers want to add new features or fix bugs, they work on different branches that are separate from the main codebase. Version control lets people work together, keep track of changes, and go back to earlier versions if something goes wrong.

2. Integration that is always going on

    automatic Builds: When changes to the code are pushed to the repository, an automatic build process is started to compile the code and make artifacts that can be run.

    Automated Testing: Unit tests and integration tests are some of the automated tests that are run to make sure that the changes to the code are right. Any tests that fail send feedback to developers.

    Rapid Feedback: CI gives workers quick feedback by finding problems with integration and failed tests early in the development process. This makes it possible to solve problems quickly.

    Version Control: CI uses version control systems to keep track of changes to code. This makes sure that changes don't interfere with each other and that code changes are easily integrated.

3. Deployment that repeats itself

    Automation: CD pipelines make the deployment process automatic, so there are no more steps that need to be done by hand. This lowers the chance of mistakes that happen during deployment.

    Plans for Deployment: To lower the risks and downtime of

deployment, CD methods often use plans such as blue-green deployment or canary releases.

**Rollback Mechanisms:** If there are problems or failures during deployment, CD pipelines can instantly roll back to a stable version. This keeps downtime to a minimum and keeps users as happy as possible.

**Staging Environments:** Code changes are often sent to staging environments by CD processes before they are sent to production. This lets more testing and evaluation happen in a setting that is very similar to production.

4. Feedback and monitoring all the time

**Real-Time Monitoring:** Monitoring tools keep track of how well an application is running, how resources are being used, how many errors are happening, and how users are interacting with it in real time.

**Alerting:** Monitoring tools can send out alerts based on set limits or strange behavior, letting teams know about problems that need to be fixed right away.

**Feedback Loops:** Monitoring data is used to help with development by guiding further changes, bug fixes, and efforts to make things run more smoothly.

**Analyzing logs:** This is the process of gathering and studying information about problems and actions taken by users in a program in order to fix them.

**Performance Optimization:** Ongoing tracking finds places where performance can be improved, which lets teams fix problems like slowdowns and inefficiency before they happen.

The CI/CD workflow's most important rules

1. Computerization

    CI/CD is based on automation. It means getting rid of human, error-prone steps in the software delivery process by using tools, scripts, and automated processes. Automation makes sure that the work is done quickly, consistently, and the same way every time.

2. Integration That Never Stops

    Continuous Integration stresses that changes to code should be added to a shared source often and automatically. This keeps code from getting out of date, makes it easier for people to work together, and finds interface problems early on.

3. Deploying all the time

    Continuous Deployment adds to CI by automating the process of putting changes to code into different settings. CD makes sure that changes to the code are released consistently and reliably, which lowers the chance of problems with deployment.

4. Tracking changes

   Version control is necessary to keep track of the past of code changes, manage changes to the code, and allow collaboration. Code repositories are put together and managed with version control tools like Git.

5. Testing that is done automatically

   An important part of CI/CD is automated testing. It has unit tests, integration tests, and other types of tests that make sure changes to the code are right and work as expected. With automated testing, bugs can be found early on in the development process.

6. Feedback and monitoring all the time

Monitoring production settings all the time gives you real-time information about how applications are running and how users are behaving. Monitoring gives teams information that helps them make more changes and solve problems quickly.

Pros of the CI/CD Workflow

1. Shorter time between development cycles

   CI/CD gets rid of manual steps that slow down the development process and speeds up the testing, deployment, and merging of code. This means that development processes are shorter and new features are released more quickly.

2. Better quality software

   Bugs and problems are caught early in the development process by automated testing and continuous merging. This leads to better software quality and fewer bugs in production.

3. Less work done by hand

   With CI/CD pipelines, boring and error-prone tasks are done automatically, so workers don't have to do them by hand and can focus on more creative and important tasks.

4. Working together more

   Regular integration and automated tests make it easier for developers to work together. Integration problems are found early, which makes the creation process go more smoothly.

5. Better safety measures

   CI/CD pipelines can have security checks added to them to look

for bugs in the code and make sure it meets security standards. Concerns about security are dealt with ahead of time.
6. Less time to market

CI/CD speeds up development cycles and automates tasks so that organizations can give people new features and updates more quickly. This shorter time to market can give you an edge over your competitors.

Tech and Tools for CI/CD

Jenkins is an open-source automation service that makes it easier to test, build, and release changes to code.

Travis CI is a continuous integration service that runs in the cloud and makes testing and deploying projects stored on sites like GitHub easy.

CircleCI is yet another CI/CD tool that runs in the cloud and automates the testing and deployment process.

This is GitLab CI/CD, a combined CI/CD platform that is part of the GitLab DevOps toolchain. It has version control, CI, CD, and more all in one app.

GitHub Actions is an automation tool for CI/CD workflows that works with GitHub accounts.

Docker and Kubernetes are technologies for containerization and container orchestration that are often used in CI/CD to consistently package and launch apps.

The CI/CD method is a revolutionary way to make software. It speeds up the whole process of delivering software, from testing and integrating code to deploying it and keeping an eye on it. CI/CD workflows are based on key ideas like automation, continuous integration, and continuous deployment. They offer many benefits, such as shorter development cycles, better software quality, better collaboration, and shorter time-to-market.

Companies use a range of tools and technologies, each tailored to their own needs and preferences, to successfully adopt CI/CD. By using the CI/CD process, development teams can not only get software to customers faster, but they can also quickly adapt to changing market needs and stay ahead of the competition in today's constantly changing software world.

# Chapter 2

## Cloud Infrastructure for CI/CD

Companies are using cloud technology more and more to speed up their Continuous Integration and Continuous Deployment (CI/CD) processes in today's fast-paced software development world. Cloud computing lets development teams build, test, and release software more quickly by giving them scalability, freedom, and a wide range of services. We will talk about the role of cloud infrastructure in CI/CD, as well as its perks, best practices, and important things to keep in mind.

**Learning About Cloud Infrastructure for CI/CD**

When you use cloud computing tools and services to help with the CI/CD workflow, this is called "cloud infrastructure for CI/CD." Using cloud providers' infrastructure, platforms, and tools to simplify and improve different stages of software development, such as testing and integrating code to deploying and keeping an eye on things, is what this method is all about.

**Important Parts of CI/CD Cloud Infrastructure:**

Cloud service companies offer virtual machines (VMs), container services, and serverless computing platforms that can be used to do things like writing code, testing it, and putting it into production.

**Storage:** Artifacts, logs, and other data created during the CI/CD process can be stored reliably and on a large scale using cloud storage services.

**Networking:** Load balancers and cloud networks make it possible for different parts of the CI/CD process to talk to each other in a safe and efficient way.

**Managed Services:** Certain cloud service companies offer managed databases, message queues, and other services that can be added to the CI/CD process.

**Containers:** Containerization systems, such as Docker and Kubernetes, are often used to package apps and make sure they work the same way in all environments.

**Serverless computing:** Platforms that don't run servers, like AWS Lambda and Azure Functions, let developers run code when certain events happen without having to manage servers.

**Monitoring and Logging:** Monitoring and logging services are available from cloud companies to keep an eye on the performance of applications, find problems, and learn more about the CI/CD process.

Why using cloud infrastructure for CI/CD is a good idea

**Scalability:** It's easy to make cloud tools bigger or smaller to handle different amounts of work. This makes sure that CI/CD processes can handle more work when development is at its busiest.

Cloud providers give a lot of different services and tools that can be changed to fit your CI/CD needs. Teams can pick the parts that work best for their process.

**Cost-effectiveness:** With cloud infrastructure, businesses only pay for the tools they use, which lowers the cost of the infrastructure. Costs can also be cut through automation and optimization.

**Global Reach:** Cloud companies have data centers in many parts of the world. This lets businesses put applications and CI/CD pipelines closer to the people they want to use them, which cuts down on latency.

**Automation:** Infrastructure as Code (IaC) tools like Terraform and AWS CloudFormation can be used to handle cloud infrastructure. This automation makes sure that settings are always the same.

**Security and Compliance:** Cloud providers offer strong security measures and compliance certifications, which makes it easier for businesses to keep their equipment safe.

**Disaster Recovery:** Cloud companies offer disaster recovery services, such as data backup and redundancy, to make sure that CI/CD pipelines are always available, even if something goes wrong.

**Integration Options:** Many cloud companies offer seamless connections with well-known CI/CD platforms and tools, which makes it easier to use cloud infrastructure in current processes.

The best ways to set up cloud infrastructure in CI/CD

1. **Make your goals clear:**
   Set clear goals and standards for your CI/CD process before you move to or adopt cloud infrastructure. Write down the exact problems you want to solve and the results you want to see.
2. **Pick the Right Cloud Service Provider:**
   Choose a cloud provider that fits the wants, goals, and technology

stack of your business. Some well-known cloud service companies are Amazon Web Services (AWS), Microsoft Azure, Google Cloud Platform (GCP), and more.

3. Make your designs scalable:
Make CI/CD systems that can be expanded horizontally to handle more work. Use cloud providers' auto-scaling tools to make sure you're getting the most out of your resources.

4. Use Infrastructure as Code (IaC):
To set up and run cloud systems, use IaC tools. Version control, repeatability, and automation of infrastructure providing are all possible with this method.

5. Safety and following the rules:
Put security first by following best practices for managing identities and access, encrypting data, and keeping your network safe. Make sure that the rules and guidelines for the business are followed.

6. Making the most of resources:
To keep prices down, review and improve cloud resources on a regular basis. Keep an eye on how resources are being used and change settings based on what is needed.

7. Set up automated testing environments:
Using cloud technology, automate the process of setting up and removing testing environments. This makes sure that testing settings are always the same and can be set up whenever needed.

8. Putting things in boxes:
Think about using tools like Docker for containerization and Kubernetes for container orchestration. Containers make it easier to launch apps and make sure they work the same way in all environments.

9. Watching and keeping records:
Set up strong monitoring and logging tools to keep an eye on the health and performance of CI/CD pipelines and cloud-based apps.

10. Integration and deployment that happen all the time:
Net vb
Copy the code
You can automate code integration, testing, and deployment by adding CI/CD tools and techniques to your cloud infrastructure. For continuous release, use tools like auto-deployment.

11. Backing up and getting back:
the kotlin
Copy the code
Create thorough plans for backing up and restoring important CI/CD

parts, making sure that data is safe and that you can recover from disasters.
12. **Record keeping and training:**
Circuit Board Arduino
Copy the code
Write down how the cloud system is set up and how work is done. Make sure everyone on the team knows how the cloud-based CI/CD process works by training them.
13. **Figuring out costs:**

Net vb
Copy the code
To control and lower cloud-related costs, use cost management techniques like making budgets, using cost analysis tools, and making the best use of resources.

**Important Things to Think About for CI/CD Cloud Infrastructure**

1. **Privacy and compliance with data:**
   Make sure that your CI/CD pipelines and cloud platforms follow data privacy laws and industry-specific compliance standards, like GDPR and HIPAA.
2. **Lock-in with a vendor:**
   When you use proprietary cloud services, you should be aware that you might be locked into one seller. To lower this risk, think about multi-cloud or hybrid cloud solutions.
3. **How to keep things safe:**
   To keep private data and code safe, use strong security measures like access control, encryption, and security monitoring.
4. **Keeping costs down:**
   Pay close attention to how much cloud costs. To avoid surprise costs, use cost tracking and optimization techniques.
5. **Latency and the network:**
   If your team is spread out around the world, you should think about how running CI/CD pipelines
   in the cloud will affect network design and latency.
6. **Problems with integration:**
   Make sure that your CI/CD tools and cloud system components work together without any problems. Use the APIs and SDKs that cloud service companies offer.

7. Recovery from disasters:
   Make and try disaster recovery plans to make sure that CI/CD pipelines will still work if the cloud goes down or fails.
8. Systems that are old:
   Deal with the integration challenges that come with moving old systems and workflows to CI/CD pipelines hosted in the cloud.
9. Size of Resources:
   Make sure that cloud resources are the right size so that you don't over- or under-provision them, which can affect cost and efficiency.
10. Checking on performance:

css
Copy the code
Use thorough methods for performance tuning and monitoring to make sure

## 2.1 Understanding Cloud Services

The way people and businesses access, store, and handle data and apps has changed a lot because of cloud services. The idea of cloud services, their main features, types, advantages, and challenges will all be covered in this in-depth guide. You'll know a lot about how cloud services are changing the world of computers by the end.

### What Are Services in the Cloud?

Cloud services, which are also called "cloud computing" or just "the cloud," are a group of online computer tools and programs. Cloud service providers host and handle these tools and programs in data centers all over the world. Users don't have to rely on local servers or PCs to access and use cloud services. Instead, they use web browsers or special apps to do so.

Cloud services are a flexible and scalable way to do computing that lets people and businesses use software and computing tools on a pay-as-you-go basis. This means that businesses don't have to buy and manage expensive hardware and software that is kept on-site.

### Important Things About Cloud Services

1. Self-Service on Demand:
   Users can set up and handle services and computing resources as needed, without the service provider having to do anything. This self-service feature makes it possible to be flexible and adapt to new needs.
2. Access to a wide network:
   Cloud services can be accessed through the internet on computers,

smartphones, and tablets, among other things. This makes it easier for people to work together and be flexible from afar.
3. Sharing of resources:
Cloud service companies share computers, storage, and networks so they can serve many clients at once. These resources are dynamically given and reassigned based on demand, which makes the best use of them and saves money.
4. Rapid Swelling:
Cloud services can quickly grow or shrink to handle different amounts of work. This flexibility makes sure that users have the computer power they need, when they need it, without having too much.
5. Service that can be measured:

Users are charged depending on how much of the cloud's resources and services they actually use. This "pay-as-you-go" plan lowers the initial cost and makes payments more in line with how much you use it.

Ways to Use the Cloud

1. The first is Infrastructure as a Service (IaaS):
IaaS lets you use virtualized computer tools over the internet. The cloud gives people the chance to rent virtual machines, storage space, and networking equipment. IaaS is good for businesses that want to focus on deploying and handling their own software and apps instead of managing their own hardware.
2. PaaS (Platform as a Service):
PaaS gives you a platform with development tools, application frameworks, and runtime environments that you can use to create, launch, and oversee apps. When writers use PaaS, they can focus on writing code while the platform takes care of infrastructure and scalability. Google App Engine, Heroku, and Microsoft Azure App Service are all well-known PaaS companies.
3. SaaS (Software as a Service):
SaaS lets you subscribe to fully working software apps that you can access over the internet. People can use web browsers to access these apps without having to install or update software on their own computers. Google Workspace, Microsoft 365, and Salesforce are all well-known examples of SaaS.
4. Serve as a Service (FaaS) or Serverless:
FaaS, which is also called "serverless computing," lets writers run code when certain events happen without having to manage servers.

Cloud companies give resources to run code automatically, so developers can focus on writing functions (also called "serverless" apps) that react to certain events. AWS Lambda, Azure Functions, and Google Cloud Functions are all well-known FaaS options.

5. CaaS (Container as a Service):
CaaS offers a tool for managing and deploying containerized apps called a container orchestration platform. Containers keep apps and their dependencies in a consistent environment. This makes it easier to launch and scale apps in different settings. A lot of people use Kubernetes as a CaaS tool.

6. Storage the way you want it:

You can rent storage space. gives storage options that can be changed and expanded in the cloud. Users can back up their data, files, and info and get it back whenever they need to. Amazon S3 and Google Cloud store are two examples of object store services.

Why cloud services are good

1. Savings on costs:
With cloud services, you don't have to spend a lot of money on computers and data centers. Users only pay for the services and resources they use. This lowers the cost of infrastructure and makes prices more predictable.

2. Being scalable:
With cloud services, you can change the size of your tools based on how much you need them. This scalability makes sure that users can handle changes in their jobs without having to make too many resources available.

3. Being flexible and quick:
Users can pick from a lot of different computing tools and services when they use cloud services. Users are able to quickly change their needs and try out new technologies.

4. Easy access:
With an internet link, you can use cloud services from almost anywhere. This makes it easier for people to work from home and for teams that are spread out to work together.

5. Dependability and back-ups:
Most cloud service companies have strong data centers with multiple backup systems and redundant infrastructure. This lowers the chance of losing data and experiencing downtime.

6. Updating and care that happen automatically:
   Users don't have to worry about software updates, security patches, and regular maintenance because cloud companies take care of these tasks.
7. Safety:
   Cloud service companies spend money on advanced security measures and compliance certifications that make data more private and protect it better.
8. Recovery from disasters:

A lot of cloud services come with emergency recovery plans that back up and duplicate your data in case something bad happens.

Problems and Things to Think About

Cloud services have many benefits, but they also come with some challenges and things to think about.

1. Worries about safety:
   Cloud security is the job of both the customer and the service provider. Users must use strong security measures and follow best practices for keeping data and apps safe.
2. Follow-through:
   When businesses use cloud services, they need to make sure they follow data privacy laws and industry-specific rules, which may be different in each area.
3. Lock-in with a vendor:
   It can be hard and expensive to switch from one cloud service to another. Users should be aware of the risk of being locked into one vendor and think about multi-cloud or hybrid cloud plans.
4. The cost of sending data:
   It may cost more to send and receive a lot of data to and from the cloud, especially if your speed is limited.
5. Power outages and downtime:
   The goal of cloud service companies is high availability, but sometimes there may be problems. To keep downtime to a minimum, users should have emergency recovery plans in place.
6. Changes in performance:

When cloud tools are shared, performance can vary, especially when they are being used a lot. As users, you should keep an eye on and improve how resources are used.Cloud services have changed the way we do computing by giving us access to a wide range of tools and apps that can be changed and scaled up or down as needed. Cloud services have the tools and features to meet your computing needs, whether you're an individual looking to keep files, a startup building a web app, or a business trying to make the most of your IT infrastructure.

Individuals and businesses can make smart choices about how to use the cloud to drive innovation, cut costs, and make their computing settings more flexible and responsive by learning about the main features, types, benefits, and challenges of cloud services. Cloud services will continue to be at the cutting edge of modern computing, shaping how we work, collaborate, and come up with new ideas in a world that is becoming more and more linked.

## 2.2 Choosing the Right Cloud Provider

Businesses and people who want to use the power of cloud computing must make a very important choice: which cloud service to use. There are many cloud service providers that offer different services, so it's important to make an informed choice that fits your wants and goals. This detailed guide will talk about the things you should think about when picking a cloud service, the major players in the market, and the best ways to make the right choice.

**Why picking the right cloud provider is important**

**Cost-effectiveness:** Different cloud providers have different pricing plans, and picking the right one can help you save money and avoid spending more than you planned.

**Performance:** How well your cloud company does can affect how fast and reliably your apps and services work.

**protection and Compliance:** The most important things are data protection and following the rules. The cloud company you choose should meet your needs for security and compliance.

**Scalability:** Being able to easily add or remove resources is important for adapting to changing tasks.

**Offerings of Services:** The range and depth of services and tools a cloud provider provides can affect how well you can build, launch, and manage apps.

**Support and Dependability:** The level of customer service and the provider's track record of uptime are very important for making sure that your applications are always available.

**Things to Think About When Picking a Cloud Service Provider**

1. **Types of Services:**
   A lot of different cloud service companies offer many different services, such as computing, storage, databases, machine learning, the

internet of things (IoT), and more. Think about what your project needs and make sure the service company can meet those needs.

2. **Prices and how costs are set:**
   Find out how the service charges for things like pay-as-you-go, reserved instances, and spot instances. Figure out how much it will cost based on how you plan to use it and your budget.

3. **Reliability and performance:**
   Find out where the provider's data centers are located, how their networks are set up, and how long they promise uptime. Think about the latency and network speed of the people you want to reach.

4. **Safety and following the rules:**
   Check to see if the service has the right security measures, certifications, and adherence to industry standards like GDPR and HIPAA. Check to see how they handle managing identities, encrypting data, and controlling access.

5. **Being scalable:**
   Check to see how easy it is to add or remove resources as needed to meet changing tasks. Look for tools that can make the best use of resources, such as auto-scaling.

6. **Presence in the area:**
   Think about how far the cloud service can reach. Pick one with data centers in places where your target audience is or where the data residency rules are.

7. **Lock-in with a vendor:**
   Check to see how likely it is that you will be stuck with a certain service. Some providers have options that are easier to use and take with you than others.

8. **Agreements for support and service level (SLAs):**
   Check out the provider's SLAs, response times, and customer service choices. Find out what
   kind of help you can expect if there are problems or outages.

9. **Integration and the ecosystem:**
   Think about the ecosystem of tools and third-party services that the site offers. It's important that it works with the tools and processes you already have.

10. **Community and Record Keeping:**
    Check to see if there are fan groups, forums, and a lot of information available. A strong community can offer help and useful information.

11. **Concerns about compliance and the law:**
    Make sure that the option you choose is legal and meets the regulations that apply to your business and area.

12. Costs of Data Transfer and Bandwidth:
    Keep in mind the prices of data transfer and bandwidth, especially if you plan to send a lot of data.
13. Recovery from disasters and backups:
    Check out the provider's backup and disaster recovery choices, such as how they handle data redundancy and recovery.
14. New ideas and a plan:

Think about how committed the source is to new ideas and how often they add new services and features.

Big Cloud Service Providers

1. AWS, or Amazon Web Services:
   AWS is one of the world's biggest and best cloud service providers. It has a lot of different services, such as Amazon EC2 (computing), Amazon S3 (storage), and AWS Lambda (serverless). AWS is a great choice for global deployments because it has data centers in many places around the world.
2. Azure from Microsoft:
   Microsoft Azure is well known in the business world and offers a wide range of services. Azure Virtual Machines, Azure Blob Storage, and Azure Functions are some of the things it offers. It works well with Windows Server, SQL Server, and other Microsoft tools.
3. GCP (Google Cloud Platform):
   Google Cloud is known for its ability to analyze data and learn from it. Google Cloud Platform (GCP) has features like Google Compute Engine, Google Cloud Storage, and Google Cloud Functions. Google's world network infrastructure is designed to work quickly.
4. The IBM Cloud:
   IBM Cloud has a mix of platform, hardware, and software services. It is known for focusing on hybrid and multi-cloud solutions, which means that companies with different IT environments can use it.
5. The Oracle Cloud:
   Oracle Cloud offers cloud services that are designed to work with business systems and programs. It provides Oracle Cloud Infrastructure (OCI), Oracle Autonomous Database, and other services that are geared toward security and high uptime.
6. The Alibaba Cloud:
   Alibaba Cloud is a big cloud service provider in Asia, and it's been growing its business around the world. It has a number of AI and

data analytics tools as well as services like Elastic Compute Service (ECS) and Object Storage Service (OSS).

7. Heroku for Salesforce:
Salesforce's Heroku platform provides cloud services, with a focus on Platform as a Service (PaaS) for building and deploying apps.

8. The DigitalOcean:
DigitalOcean is known for being easy to use and nice to developers. It offers cloud technology that is mostly focused on Kubernetes and virtual machines (Droplets).

9. Technology from Rackspace:
Rackspace provides managed cloud services, which make it a good choice for businesses that need help handling their cloud resources.

10. The Tencent Cloud:

Tencent Cloud is a well-known cloud service company in Asia. It provides many services and has a lot of experience with entertainment and games.

How to Pick the Best Cloud Service Provider

**Check Your Needs:** To begin, look at what your project needs, such as computing power, storage space, the ability to grow, and compliance. It will help you cut down your choices if you know what you need.

**Do a Proof of Concept (PoC):** Before making a full commitment, you might want to do a PoC with one of the providers you've chosen to see how their services work in the real world.

**Think about a Multi-Cloud or Hybrid Strategy:** A multi-cloud or hybrid cloud strategy could help you avoid being locked into one provider and get the best performance for certain use cases, depending on your needs.

**Get Advice from Experts:** Talk to cloud experts, architects, or consultants to learn more about your unique needs and challenges.

**Plan for Data Migration:** If you're moving current data and applications, make sure you have a clear plan for data migration and think about how much it will cost.

**Review Pricing and Cost Management:** To keep costs down and avoid shocks on your monthly bill, keep an eye on and improve how you use the cloud on a regular basis.

**Focus on Security and Compliance:** Pay close attention to the encryption options, security features, and compliance certifications that are important to your business.

Explore the Ecosystem and Integration: Look into the third-party tools, relationships, and integrations that can make your cloud experience better.

Find Customer Reviews and Case Studies: Read customer reviews and case studies to learn how the cloud provider's services have helped other businesses.

Keep Up: To get the most out of the newest features, stay up to date on the cloud provider's plan and new services.

In today's digital world, picking the right cloud provider is a smart choice that can have a big effect on the success of your business. By giving your needs some thought, looking at the things this guide talks about, and keeping up with how the cloud industry is changing, you can make a choice that fits your needs and helps you succeed in the world of cloud computing. With the right cloud partner, you can develop, grow, and do well in the digital age. This is true whether you choose a big player like AWS, Azure, or GCP or a more specialized provider.

## 2.3 Setting Up Cloud Environments for CI/CD

CI/CD, or Continuous Integration and Continuous Deployment, is now an important part of modern software development. It helps teams make software faster, more reliable, and better. A key step toward these goals is setting up cloud platforms for CI/CD. This detailed guide will look at the best ways to set up cloud environments that work with CI/CD processes, as well as important things to keep in mind.

### How to Understand the Part of Cloud Environments in CI/CD

Code Integration: When developers make changes to code, they commit them to a version control system like Git. This starts the CI/CD process.

Build and Test: The CI/CD system gets the code, builds the app, and runs a bunch of automated tests to make sure the code is good.

Deployment: The CI/CD system sends the app to a staging or production location once all of the tests pass.

Monitoring and Feedback: Continuous monitoring tools are often built into the cloud to give real-time feedback on problems and how well applications are running.

For fast, reliable, and automated software delivery, you need to set up a strong cloud setting that fits with your CI/CD goals.

### How to set up cloud environments for CI/CD in the best way

Infrastructure as Code (IaC): Use IaC tools like AWS CloudFormation or Terraform to describe and set up cloud resources automatically. This makes sure that your cloud setting is consistent, can be used again, and has version control.

**Separate settings:** Keep development, testing, staging, and production settings separate from each other to keep changes separate and lower the risk of production failures.

**Containerization:** To package apps and the files they need, use containerization tools like Docker. Container orchestration platforms, such as Kubernetes, can make it easier to handle apps that run in containers.

**Automated Provisioning:** Use scripts or infrastructure automation tools to make the provisioning of cloud services automatic. This cuts down on the amount of manual setup and the chance of making a mistake.

**Immutable Infrastructure:** Think of cloud resources as "immutable," which means that they are replaced instead of changed. This method makes changes and rollbacks easier.

**Scalability:** Make sure that your cloud system can grow horizontally to handle different amounts of work. Set up auto-scaling based on data for how resources are being used.

**High Availability (HA):** Use HA architectures to make sure that your service can still be accessed and used even if some of its parts stop working. When you need to, use load balancers and backups.

**Security:** To keep your cloud setting safe, use best practices like controlling who can access it, encrypting data, and scanning for security holes. Check and change security settings on a regular basis.

**Monitoring and Logging:** To learn more about your apps' health and performance, use monitoring and logging services that are built for the cloud. Set up alerts for important events.

**Continuous merging:** To automate code merging, testing, and deployment, connect your CI/CD tool to the cloud. Jenkins, Travis CI, GitLab CI/CD, and CircleCI are all well-known CI/CD tools.

**Blue-Green Deployments:** Use blue-green deployments to keep updating as low-impact as possible. To do this, you need to launch a new version of your app along with the old one and then switch traffic to the new version once it has been checked.

**Environment Variables:** Use environment variables or secret management services from the cloud source to keep track of private data like API keys and database credentials.

**Cost Management:** To avoid unexpected costs, use cost tracking and improvement techniques. Use the cloud's budgeting and cost research tools.

Tips for Setting Up CI/CD Environments in the Cloud

**Single Cloud Provider:** Many businesses choose a single cloud provider (like AWS, Azure, or

Google Cloud) to make management easier and use the ecosystem of services and connections that the provider offers. This method can work well for groups that have specific platform needs.

**Multi-Cloud:** Some businesses choose a multi-cloud approach to avoid being locked into one vendor and make their systems more resilient. Spreading work across several cloud companies lowers the chance of a single point of failure. Multi-cloud environments, on the other hand, can be harder to handle.

**Hybrid Cloud:** Companies use a hybrid cloud approach to mix on-premises infrastructure with resources in the cloud. This method might work for companies that have old systems or have to follow certain rules.

For certain tasks or workloads, you might want to look into serverless computing tools like AWS Lambda, Azure Functions, or Google Cloud Functions. For event-driven apps, serverless can make managing the system easier and lower costs.

**controlled Services:** Every chance you get, use the cloud provider's controlled services. Managed databases, message queues, and serverless platforms can make upkeep easier and cut down on operational costs.

Setting up your CI/CD pipeline as code can be done with tools like Jenkinsfile, GitLab CI/CD YAML, or AWS CodePipeline templates. Versioning and consistency are easier to achieve when you store your CI/CD settings as code.

**Testing settings:** Set up and take down testing settings in the cloud automatically. This makes sure that testing settings are always the same and can be set up whenever needed.

**Culture of DevOps:** Encourage your company to have a culture of DevOps by stressing the importance of dialogue and working together between the development and operations teams. Changing this way of thinking is necessary for CI/CD to work.

Important Things to Think About for Certain Cloud Providers

1. AWS, or Amazon Web Services:
   AWS has a huge number of services, so it can be used for many different things.
   AWS Elastic Beanstalk makes it easier to launch and scale applications.
   Event-driven apps can use serverless computing with AWS Lambda.
   Both AWS CodePipeline and AWS CodeDeploy have built-in CI/CD features.
2. Azure from Microsoft:
   Azure DevOps offers a full range of CI/CD services and tools.
   Azure Kubernetes Service (AKS) makes it easier to run Kubernetes

groups.

Azure Functions lets you do computing without a computer.

With Azure Logic Apps, you can automate your process.

3. GCP (Google Cloud Platform):

Google Kubernetes Engine (GKE) is a service for managing Kubernetes containers.

Cloud Functions lets you do work without a server.

Cloud Build has a built-in CI/CD tool.

Google Cloud Composer can help you automate your work flow.

4. Other Service Providers:

Check out the CI/CD and DevOps tools and services that other cloud companies, such as IBM Cloud, Oracle Cloud, and DigitalOcean, offer to see if they meet your needs.

Setting up CI/CD environments in the cloud is an important part of current software development because it makes automation, scalability, and reliability possible. You can set up a cloud setting that works well for your CI/CD workflow by following best practices, strategies, and taking certain cloud provider features into account.

Remember that the cloud environment and tools you choose should fit with the goals of your company, the needs of your applications, and the infrastructure you already have. A well-designed cloud environment can speed up software delivery, improve collaboration, and spur innovation in your development processes, no matter if you choose a single cloud provider, a multi-cloud approach, or serverless computing.

## 2.4 Cost Considerations and Optimization

Cost control is an important part of cloud computing. Even though the cloud is scalable, flexible, and cost-effective, it can also cost you more than you thought if you don't manage it well. This complete guide will go over the main cost factors and optimization methods for cloud computing. This will help people and businesses make smart choices and get the most out of their investments (ROI).

### Why managing costs is important in cloud computing

**Scalability:** The cloud lets you change the size of your resources based on your needs. However, if you don't keep an eye on this, it can cost you more than it needs to.

**Complexity:** Cost tracking and optimization can be hard because there are so many cloud services, pricing models, and areas to choose from.

**Misconfiguration:** If you don't set up cloud resources correctly, you might end up overprovisioning them, which wastes resources and raises your bills.

**Lack of Visibility:** It's hard to know how resources are being used and where costs are coming from without proper tracking and cost analysis.

**Idle Resources:** Over time, leaving resources working when they're not needed can cost a lot of money.

**Costs of Data Transfer:** There may be extra costs for moving data between cloud services, areas, or external networks.

Businesses must be able to control their costs well if they want to get the most out of cloud computing without spending too much. Let's talk about the most important things to think about and ways to keep cloud costs down.

What You Need to Know About Cloud Computing Costs

1. **Choose a cloud service:**
   Pick the right cloud service for the work you need to do. There are different pricing systems for different services, such as virtual machines, serverless, and managed databases. Check to see which services meet the needs of your program the best.
2. **Ways to Set Prices:**
   Find out how the cloud service charges for things like on-demand instances, reserved instances, spot instances, and pay-as-you-go options. Pick the pricing plan that works best for your budget and how you usually use it.
3. **Size of Resources:**
   Make sure that the size of your cloud tools is right for your work. Too much provisioning costs money that isn't needed, and too little provisioning can hurt efficiency. To make changes as needed, use resource tracking and scaling.
4. **Tags for resources:**
   You can tag your cloud services with metadata that helps with billing. This makes it easier to keep track of prices and helps you give the right amount of money to projects or departments.
5. **In automation:**
   Use automation tools and processes to set up and remove resources based on demand.
   Automation makes it less likely that resources will be left going when they aren't needed.
6. **Instances that have been reserved:**
   If you know how much work you will have, you might want to buy reserved instances or contracts. If you agree to these choices for a longer time, you will save money.
7. **Look for Instances:**
   Spot instances, which you can get from AWS, Azure, and GCP, are

best for non-critical, fault-tolerant tasks. When compared to on-demand instances, spot instances are a big money saver.
8. **Making the most of storage:**
To lower storage costs, use data lifecycle management and object storage rules. Find old data that you don't need and either delete it or put it in a backup.
9. **The cost of sending data:**
Keep in mind the prices of data transfer, especially if your app needs to send a lot of data between regions or to networks outside of your company. When it makes sense, use a Content Delivery Network (CDN).
10. **Tracking and analysis:**
Use tracking and analytics services that are built for the cloud to learn more about how resources are being used and how costs are changing over time. Set up alerts to find strange things and possible cost overruns.
11. **Capacity Set Aside:**

To save money on database prices, you might want to use Reserved Capacity for services like Amazon RDS on platforms like AWS.

Strategies for lowering cloud costs

1. **Make a clear budget to begin:**
Make a clear budget for the money you will spend on the cloud. This budget should be in line with the financial goals and limits of your company.
2. **Monitoring all the time:**
Keep an eye on your cloud resources and prices all the time. Track costs and usage with cloud service dashboards, third-party tools, and your own scripts.
3. **Sharing the costs:**
Use tags and labels to correctly assign costs to teams, departments, or projects. This makes it easier to see where improvements need to be made.
4. **Make resources your own:**
Check how the resources are being used on a regular basis and change the size or type of resources as needed. Auto-scaling lets you change resources on the fly based on demand.
5. **Bring together resources:**
Find tools that aren't being used or are just sitting there, and combine workloads where you can. One way to do this is to use

serverless computing or combine multiple virtual machines onto a single instance.
6. Make use of spot instances and discounts:
Cloud companies offer spot instances, committed use discounts, and other similar services that can help you save money on non-production or peak workloads.
7. Make serverless work:
For certain tasks or jobs, serverless computing might be a good option. Serverless platforms handle and scale resources automatically, so you don't have to do it by hand.
8. Backing up and tiering data:
Set up rules for data archiving and tiering to move data that isn't used very often to cheaper storage levels, like cold or archive storage.
9. Use Auto-Scaling and Auto-Pause:
Use the auto-pause and auto-scaling tools in databases to save money when they're not being used and to adjust the resources based on demand.
10. Reduce the cost of your network:
Optimize network routes and use a content delivery network (CDN) for static files to keep data transfer costs as low as possible.
11. Use tools for cost management:
Cloud service companies offer cost management tools and dashboards that show how much you're spending and suggest ways to cut costs. Make good use of these tools.
12. Teach and train your teams:
Spend money on teaching your teams in cloud cost optimization. Teach the finance, operations, and development teams the best ways to control cloud costs.
13. Set up budget alerts:
Set up budget alerts to let you know when your spending goes over certain limits. This early warning method helps you quickly fix the problem.
14. Review and improve on a regular basis:

Cost management is a process that never ends. Plan to look at your cloud costs on a regular basis and make changes as needed to make sure they fit with your budget and goals.To get the most out of cloud computing while keeping costs under control, you need to be able to effectively handle and optimize costs. People and businesses can find the best mix between innovation and cost control by learning about key cost factors, putting cost optimization strategies into action, and using cloud-native cost management tools. Cost optimization in the cloud is an ongoing process. If you keep an eye on and make changes to your cloud resources, you will save money in the long run and get the most out of your cloud investments.

# Chapter 3

Designing CI/CD Pipelines in the Cloud

Pipelines for Continuous Integration and Continuous Deployment (CI/CD) are now an important part of how software is developed today. They let teams automate the process of building, testing, and deploying apps, which speeds up development, improves quality, and speeds up release to production. Using cloud computing tools for CI/CD pipelines makes them scalable, flexible, and reliable. We will talk about best practices, strategies, and important things to think about when building CI/CD pipelines in the cloud in this detailed guide.

**The Beginning**

**Faster Development Cycles:** Automation cuts down on human involvement, which speeds up the time it takes to go from committing code to deploying it in production.

**Better Quality:** Code changes are carefully checked when automated testing and validation methods are used, which leads to better software.

**Efficient Collaboration:** CI/CD encourages the development, testing, and operations teams to work together, which leads to a mindset of shared responsibility.

**Lower Risk:** When launches and rollbacks are done automatically, mistakes made by people are less likely to happen, and problems are found early.

**Scalability:** Cloud-based CI/CD pipelines are easy to expand to handle larger tasks and teams that work in different places.

**Why cloud-based CI/CD pipelines are better**

**Scalability:** Because cloud providers give resources on demand, your CI/CD pipeline can grow either horizontally or vertically to adapt to changing needs.

**Flexibility:** Cloud platforms offer many diverse services and connections that can be changed to fit your unique pipeline needs.

Pay-as-you-go price models let you save money by only charging you for the resources you use. This makes cloud-based CI/CD cost-effective.

**Global Reach:** Cloud companies have data centers in many parts of the world, so you can set up your CI/CD pipeline closer to the people you want to reach to get better latency.

**Security:** Cloud providers put a lot of money into security measures, which means that your CI/CD pipeline will have strong system security.

**Managed Services:** To make your CI/CD system easier to use, use managed services like databases, containers, and serverless computing.

**Ecosystems and Integration:** Cloud providers offer large groups of tools and services that work well together. This makes it easier to connect to other cloud resources and services from other companies.

**Important Parts of CI/CD Pipelines in the Cloud**

**Version Control System (VCS):** A VCS like Git is the base that lets multiple developers work together, keep track of changes, and handle the source code.

**Built and Compilation Automatically:** This part makes it possible to build the app from source code automatically. Tools like Maven, Gradle, and npm are often used.

**Automated Testing:** Unit tests, integration tests, and end-to-end tests are all types of automated tests. They make sure that changes to the code don't cause problems to happen again.

As the name suggests, an artifact repository is a place where build files, dependencies, and release packages are kept. Nexus, JFrog Artifactory, and Amazon S3 are all popular options.

**Continuous Integration Server (CI server):** A CI server, like Jenkins or GitLab CI/CD, helps with building, testing, and deploying codes.

**Automation of Deployments:** Tools like Ansible, Terraform, and Kubernetes make deployments uniform and repeatable.

**Monitoring and Logging:** Monitoring tools like Prometheus and Grafana, along with log aggregation services like Elasticsearch and Logstash, give you information about how well and how healthy your apps are.

**Notification and Alerting:** Systems like Slack, PagerDuty, or email let people know about problems and changes in the pipeline.

The best ways to set up CI/CD pipelines in the cloud

1. Controlling versions and a code repository
   To handle code changes well, use a distributed version control system (DVCS) like Git and set up ways to branch and merge.

# CLOUD-BASED CI/CD FOR SOFTWARE TEAMS ~ 63

Set up a code review method to make sure that the code is good and that team members can work together.

2. **Testing by Computer**

    Add a strong set of automated tests to your process, such as unit tests, integration tests, and end-to-end tests.

    Use testing tools like JUnit, Selenium, and Jest as part of your CI/CD process.

3. **Taking care of artifacts**

    You can store and handle dependencies, libraries, and build artifacts in an artifact repository. In this way, builds are consistent and can be done again and again.

    Use immutable artifacts to avoid version issues and make sure that builds can be done again and again.

4. **Strategies for Deployment**

    Use deployment methods like canary deployments or blue-green deployments to cut down on downtime and the chance of production problems.

    You can turn on or off certain features in production without having to change the code by using feature toggles or feature flags.

5. **Infrastructure as Code**

    To consistently set up and handle cloud resources, define infrastructure as code (IaC) using tools like Terraform or AWS CloudFormation. Keep IaC models with your application code so that you can keep track of versions and who made them.

6. **Isolation of the Environment**

    Separate the testing, staging, production, and development settings so that they don't affect each other and testing is reliable.

    Make it so that disposable test settings are automatically made and destroyed.

7. **Safety and Controlling Access**

    Code repositories, CI/CD servers, and cloud tools should all follow best practices for security.

    Control who can access CI/CD pipelines and cloud services with role-based access control (RBAC).

8. **Watching and keeping records**

    By combining tracking and logging tools, you can see how well your applications are running and find problems before they happen.

    In your CI/CD pipeline, set up alerts for important events and key performance measures.

9. **Able to grow and work in parallel**

Spread the work among several agents or runners in your CI/CD process to make it scalable.

To cut down on execution time, run test suites and build jobs in parallel.

### Getting a Cloud Service Provider

If you want to build a cloud-based CI/CD pipeline, choosing the right cloud service is very important. For well-known cloud services, here are some things to think about:

### AWS, or Amazon Web Services,

AWS has a huge community of services, such as AWS CodeBuild and AWS CodePipeline for CI/CD.

Use AWS Lambda for serverless CI/CD automation and AWS Elastic Beanstalk to make it easier to launch apps.

### Azure from Microsoft

Azure DevOps Services can be used to manage the whole CI/CD process.

Azure Functions lets you run apps without a server, and Azure Kubernetes Service (AKS) is great for containerized apps.

### Google Cloud Platform

GCP has Kubernetes Engine (GKE) for managing containers and Google Cloud Build for CI/CD.

You can use Google Cloud Functions to automate CI/CD without a computer.

### Other Cloud Service Providers

Think about cloud service providers like DigitalOcean, IBM Cloud, and Oracle Cloud based on your needs and the technology you already have.

### Service and Tools for CI/CD

For pipeline design to work well, it's important to pick the right CI/CD tools and services. These are some popular picks:

### John Jenkins

Jenkins is an open-source automation service that is widely used and has a huge collection of CI/CD plugins.

It gives you the freedom to make your own pipelines and connect them to different cloud companies and tools.

### Use GitLab CI/CD

GitLab CI/CD is built into GitLab's version control platform, which makes it easy for companies that use GitLab to handle their source code.

It works right out of the box with containerized apps and Kubernetes deploys.

### CI Travis

This is an easy-to-use CI/CD platform in the cloud called Travis CI. It works best for open-source projects stored on GitHub.

It has many build platforms, such as Linux, macOS, and Windows.

### CI Circle

CircleCI is a CI/CD tool that is built to work in the cloud and focuses on speed and ease of use.

It works well with both Docker and Kubernetes setups.

CodePipeline for AWS

AWS CodePipeline is a CI/CD service from Amazon Web Services that takes care of everything.

It works well with other AWS services and lets you set up your process in different ways.

DevOps in Azure

Azure Pipelines for CI/CD is part of Azure DevOps, which is a full platform.

It works well with Azure services and can be deployed in more than one cloud.

Build Google Cloud

A CI/CD service called Google Cloud Build is built into Google Cloud Platform.

It makes it possible for containerized applications to automatically be built and deployed.

More advanced CI/CD ideas

To improve your pipeline, think about more complicated CI/CD ideas besides the basics:

Deployments in Blue and Green

In blue-green deployments, two similar environments are set up and traffic is switched between them. This cuts down on downtime and makes rollbacks quick.

Deployments of Canary

With a canary deployment, new features or updates are slowly rolled out to a small group of people before they are made available to everyone. This method helps find problems early on and lowers the risk.

Toggles for Features

Feature toggles, which are sometimes called "feature flags," let you turn on or off certain features in production without changing the code. This helps with faster testing and limited releases of new features.

Tests A and B

A/B testing is the process of contrasting two versions (A and B) of an app to find the better one. The deployment of A/B tests and data collection can be done automatically by CI/CD processes.

CI/CD without servers

For CI/CD automation jobs like running tests, deploying code, or doing code reviews, serverless computing is the way to go. Serverless tasks are cost-effective and can grow as needed.

Setting up a CI/CD pipeline

Setting up, managing, and running the different steps of a CI/CD workflow is called CI/CD pipeline orchestration. For good arrangement, here are some things to think about:

**Pipelines in order**

In sequential pipelines, the stages are put in a straight line, and each step depends on the success of the one before it.

This method works well for small teams and easy workflows.

**Pipes in parallel**

Parallel pipelines run multiple stages at the same time, which lets you get input faster and cut down on build times.

When you have jobs that can be done separately, like unit tests for different parts, use parallelism.

**Fan-In and Fan-Out Pipelines**

Fan-in pipelines combine the outputs of several source sets or branches into a single pipeline so that they can be tested and integrated.

Fan-out pipelines split up work and send it to different settings, which lets testing happen at the same time in different setups.

**Pipelines with Conditions**

You can use conditional logic in your pipeline to start certain steps or jobs based on certain conditions, like branch names, commit messages, or environment variables.

With conditionals, you can change how the system acts in different situations.

**Pipelines That Change**

You can be flexible and adaptable by using dynamic pipelines to create and run pipeline steps based on data or runtime conditions.

Dynamic streams work well for projects that are complicated and change over time.

It is necessary to design CI/CD processes in the cloud in order to get faster development cycles, better software quality, and faster deployments. Companies can build strong and expandable CI/CD pipelines that work for them by following best practices, thinking about advanced ideas, and picking the right cloud service and CI/CD tools.

Remember that designing a CI/CD workflow is not a one-time thing; it's an ongoing process of making it better and better. Review and change your pipeline often to keep up with new technologies, standards, and best practices.

In the end, a well-thought-out CI/CD process in the cloud is an important part of modern software development because it helps your company be more flexible, work together, and come up with new ideas.

## 3.1 Building Blocks of CI/CD Pipelines

In the fast-paced world of software development today, it's more important than ever to release software quickly and reliably. CI/CD systems, which stand for Continuous Integration and Continuous Deployment, have become important tools for reaching this goal. Building, testing, and deploying software are all automated by CI/CD pipelines. This lets companies offer high-quality software more quickly and consistently. This article talks about what CI/CD pipelines are made of, the important parts that make them work, and how they are used in current software development.

### Change Control

Version control is the most important part of any CI/CD process. It keeps track of changes made by writers and stores source code in one place. Version control systems like Git and SVN make it easy for teams to work together, keep track of changes, and make sure that the code is stable. Teams can make a single source of truth for their codebase by using version control. This makes it easier to handle changes and add them to the pipeline.

### Automation of Builds

For CI/CD to work, the first step is automated builds. They use the version control system to get the source code and then turn it into software that can be run. This process is automated by build tools like Jenkins, Travis CI, and CircleCI. This means that the code can be turned into a working app without any help from a person. Early in the development process, automated builds find compilation mistakes. This lowers the chance of bugs and other problems.

### Testing All the Time

Tests are an important part of any software development process. Continuous testing in CI/CD pipelines means constantly running a set of tests, such as unit tests, integration tests, and acceptance tests. These tests help find problems and make sure that changes to the code don't cause new ones. Automated testing tools like JUnit, Selenium, and Postman let developers run tests quickly and consistently, giving them instant feedback on the quality of the code.

### Management of Artifacts

After the code has been built and checked, it needs to be saved as an artifact and given a version number. These artifacts are kept in artifact management systems like Nexus Repository and Artifactory so that they can be used and shared across the company.

This makes sure that the exact version of the software that passed testing is used in the next steps of the process, which stops version mismatches and inconsistencies.

### Integration that never stops (CI)

CI is a way of working with code that pushes developers to regularly add changes to a shared repository. CI servers that are automated, like Jenkins and GitLab CI/CD, check the version control system for new code changes and automatically start the build and test process. CI helps find problems with merging early on and encourages teamwork and good code.

### Automation of deployment

Automation of release is what Continuous release (CD) is all about. Based on rules and triggers that have already been set, CD pipelines instantly move software to different environments, such as development, staging, and production. Tools for deployment automation, such as Kubernetes, Docker, and Ansible, make it possible to consistently launch applications. This lowers the chance of making mistakes and speeds up the release process.

### Playing the music

Orchestration is a key part of making sure that all the steps in the CI/CD process work together smoothly. The pipeline's acts, dependencies, and conditional logic are set out in this document. Orchestration tools, such as Apache Airflow, Kubernetes Operators, and Jenkins Pipelines, let businesses set up complicated workflows and manage the deployment process without any problems.

### Monitoring All the Time

Continuous monitoring is needed to make sure that installed applications are healthy and working well. Monitoring tools like Prometheus, Grafana, and New Relic show how applications are using resources, how well the system is running, and how users are feeling at any given time. Continuous tracking helps find problems quickly and fix them, which makes the software more reliable overall.

### Rates and feedback

CI/CD pipelines that work well have feedback loops that help teams check the code's quality and speed. The metrics and logs that are created while the process is running give us useful information about how the software works. You can use these measures to find bottlenecks, make the pipeline work better, and make decisions based on data to keep getting better.

### Peace of mind

Security is a very important issue in modern software creation. To find security holes and compliance problems early, CI/CD processes should include security checks and scans in their work. To make sure that security is part of the development process from the start, tools like SonarQube, OWASP ZAP, and Clair can be added to the chain.

### Strategies for Going Back

Even with thorough testing and automation, problems can still happen during release. It is important to have rollback plans in place to reduce downtime and lessen the effects of mistakes. Version control systems and automated rollback methods make it easy for companies to quickly return to a stable state if there are problems during deployment.

**Keeping records and sharing knowledge**

People often forget about documentation, but it's an important part of CI/CD processes that

work well. Documentation that is clear and up to date helps everyone on the team understand how the process works, how to fix problems, and how to contribute effectively. Sharing what they know within the team makes sure that everyone is on the same page and can decide how to improve the process based on good information.

These CI/CD pipelines are very important for modern software development because they let teams make high-quality software quickly and reliably. Companies that want to speed up their development processes, improve teamwork, and stay competitive in today's fast-paced digital world need to understand how CI/CD systems are put together. Teams can build strong CI/CD pipelines that improve software delivery, cut down on errors, and eventually lead to business success by using these building blocks correctly.

3.2 Best Practices for CI/CD Pipeline Design

CI/CD systems, which stand for Continuous Integration and Continuous Deployment, are now necessary for making software today. They let teams simplify the process of making, testing, and releasing software, which speeds up the development process and makes releases better. But there is no one-size-fits-all way to make a good CI/CD system. It takes giving careful thought to the specific needs and wants of your project and organization. This article will talk about the best ways to build a CI/CD pipeline. It will cover key principles and things to think about that will help you make pipelines that are efficient, reliable, and scalable.

**Set clear goals to begin.**

It's important to set clear targets and goals before getting into the technical parts of CI/CD pipeline design. What do you want your CI/CD system to do? Are you trying to speed up development, improve the quality of the code, cut down on deployment mistakes, or do all of these things? Knowing your goals will help you make decisions during the planning process and decide which pipeline features are most important.

**Controlling versions and writing good code**

Version control is the first step in making CI/CD processes work well. Make sure that your team manages source code and keeps track of changes with a version control system like Git. Stress how important it is to write clean, stable code from the start. A CI/CD process works best when the code it uses is good. Tools that automatically analyze code and code review methods can help keep quality standards high.

**Make the pipeline more modular.**

Separate your CI/CD process into parts that can be used again and again. Every step in the pipeline should be responsible for a certain task, like making, testing, and deploying. When you use modules, it's easier to keep the process up to date and expand it as your project grows. It also supports parallel processing, which speeds up the running of the pipeline.

**Make everything automatic**

CI/CD is based on automating things. As much as possible of the process should be automated, from compiling and testing the code to deploying it and rolling it back. Automation not only saves time but also makes mistakes less likely. A lot of processing can be done with popular CI/CD tools like Jenkins, Travis CI, and GitLab CI/CD.

**Set up Isolation**

Keep your build environment separate to avoid setup and dependencies. To make build environments that can be used again and again, use containerization tools like Docker. This makes sure that builds are the same at all stages of the pipeline and in both the development and production settings.

**Early and often tests**

Add unit, integration, and acceptance tests, as well as other types of automated testing, to your CI/CD workflow. Running tests early and often helps find problems faster, which lowers the cost of solving bugs later on. Make sure all tests are done automatically and give clear feedback on how good the code is.

**Parallelization and being able to grow**

Plan your CI/CD pipeline so that it can use parallel processes. This lets you split up work between several machines or containers, which speeds up the processing time of the pipeline. Also, think about how your system can be expanded. The process should be able to handle more work as your project grows without needing major changes.

**Management of Artifacts**

Version control and traceability depend on being able to handle artifacts well. Keep all of your build files, like compiled binaries and deployable packages, in one place where you can also version them. Nexus Repository and Artifactory are two well-known artifact management tools that let you store, update, and share artifacts.

**Putting security first**

Your CI/CD process should have security built in at all times. Use tools like SonarQube and OWASP ZAP to check your code and libraries for security holes on a regular basis. Put in place security gates that stop code that isn't safe from moving through the flow. To make your system and container images safer, you should also follow best practices for security.

Environment Equal

Make sure that the environments where you create, test, and run your code are as similar as possible. This idea, called "environment parity," lowers the chance that problems will happen because of differences between surroundings. Infrastructure as Code (IaC) tools like Ansible and Terraform can help keep things consistent and make setting up environments easier.

Watching and keeping records

Make sure that your CI/CD pipeline has strong tracking and logging in place. You can find and fix problems quickly when you can see the pipeline's health and performance in real time. Monitoring and logging can be done completely with tools like Prometheus, Grafana, and the ELK stack (Elasticsearch, Logstash, and Kibana).

Government and Compliance

You might want to add compliance and governance checks to your CI/CD pipeline if you work in a regulated industry or for an organization with strict compliance standards. Set up approval, validation, and audit trails to make sure that all changes meet legal requirements before they are put into action.

Backwards and forwards

Add rollback and recovery features to your CI/CD process to be ready for anything that might happen. Having a clear rollback plan and backup procedures can help reduce downtime and the effect on users if a deployment fails or problems arise in production that were not expected.

Record keeping and training

Write down the design, methods, and best practices for your CI/CD pipeline. Make sure that everyone on the team knows how to use the system and how it works. Documentation and training that work well help the team be consistent and work together.

Always Getting Better

A CI/CD chain is not a one-time thing; it's a process that goes on all the time. Review and improve your pipeline all the time based on comments, metrics, and changing needs. Encourage your development team to always be looking for ways to do things better.

Making a CI/CD pipeline that works well is a difficult job that needs a lot of planning and thought. By following these best practices, you can make a pipeline that speeds up development, makes code better, and makes the whole process of delivering software better. Remember that CI/

CD pipeline design is not a one-size-fits-all method; it should be changed to fit your project and organization's wants and goals. You can get the most out of CI/CD and make your software development process better all the time if you use the right design concepts and tools.

### 3.3 Implementing Infrastructure as Code (IaC)

Infrastructure as Code (IaC) has changed the way businesses handle and set up their IT infrastructure. This way of doing things treats infrastructure like software, which lets you automate tasks, keep track of versions, and make things more reliable and scalable. This article will talk about the idea of IaC, its benefits, best practices, and the tools that are usually used to put it into action. This will help you figure out how to successfully add IaC to the way your business works.

### What does Infrastructure as Code (IaC) mean?

Infrastructure as Code, or IaC, is a way to manage and set up infrastructure tools using software engineering. IaC doesn't set up servers, networks, and other infrastructure parts by hand; instead, it uses code to describe and automate how these resources are set up and configured. Most of the time, this code is written in domain-specific languages or configuration management tools. It is tracked and managed using versions, just like any other software code.

IaC lets businesses describe their infrastructure as code, keep it in version control systems, and use automation to set up and manage their infrastructure resources. This method has many benefits, including making system management faster, more consistent, and more reliable.

### Pros of Putting IaC Into Action

**Automation:** IaC makes it possible to automate infrastructure jobs that are done over and over again. This cuts down on mistakes made by hand and boosts efficiency. Setting up, growing, and provisioning infrastructure can all be done automatically, which saves time and effort.

IaC makes sure that infrastructure is always provisioned and set the same way every time it's deployed. This prevents configuration drift, which happens when computers and resources change over time because of changes made by hand.

**Version Control:** Infrastructure code can be stored in repositories and given different versions. This lets teams keep track of changes, work together more efficiently, and go back to earlier settings if problems arise.

It's easy to change the size of infrastructure resources based on demand when you use IaC. To deal with changes in traffic and workloads, automated scaling rules can be set up.

**Reproducibility:** With IaC, you can use a single command or script to recreate full infrastructure environments, such as production, staging, and testing. This is very helpful for testing, development, and crisis recovery.

This is called documentation, and the infrastructure code itself is paperwork. By looking at the codebase, teams can easily understand how the system is built and set up.

**Collaboration:** IaC promotes the development and operations teams to work together. In code, developers can describe what infrastructure is needed, and operations teams can use that code to set up and handle resources.

**Optimizing costs:** IaC helps you handle costs better by letting you turn off or scale down resources when they're not needed, which lowers the cost of cloud infrastructure.

Best Practices for Putting IaC into Action

**Start out small:** Before you start to scale up, start with a specific project or a small part of your system to learn and improve your IaC processes.

**Pick Out the Right Tools:** Pick IaC frameworks and tools that fit the needs and skills of your company. Terraform, AWS CloudFormation, Azure Resource Manager, and Ansible are all popular choices.

**Versioning:** Use a versioning system, like Git, to store your IaC code. This lets you keep track of changes, work together with your team, and handle code versions well.

**Modularity:** Break up your IaC code into sections and components that can be used again and again. This makes things more consistent and makes upkeep easier.

**Documentation:** Use comments and written information in your IaC code to describe what tools and configurations are for and how they work.

**Tests:** To find mistakes quickly, use automatic tests to check your IaC code. Terratest and Kitchen-Terraform are two tools that can help you make sure that your infrastructure code works as it should.

**protection:** Make sure that your IaC code follows best practices for protection. Do not hardcode private information, use strong authentication methods, and check for security holes on a regular basis.

You should add your IaC code to your CI/CD workflow for continuous integration (CI). This makes sure that changes to the infrastructure are tried and confirmed before they are put into action.

**Immutable Infrastructure:** You might want to use the idea of immutable Infrastructure, which means that servers and other tools are replaced instead of changed. This makes things more predictable and lessens setup drift.

**Monitoring and Logging:** To learn more about your infrastructure's health and performance, set it up to watch and log events. You can keep an eye on IaC-deployed resources with tools like Prometheus and Grafana.

### Tools for Putting IaC into Action

The open-source IaC tool Terraform works with a number of cloud providers and on-premises systems. It sets up infrastructure tools and dependencies using a declarative language.

**AWS CloudFormation:** Amazon's IaC tool for setting up AWS resources is AWS CloudFormation. Templates in JSON or YAML are used to describe system stacks.

**Azure Resource Manager:** Templates for Azure Resource Manager (ARM) are used to directly describe and set up Azure resources and services.

The Google Cloud Deployment Manager program sets up and uses YAML or Jinja2 templates to set up and use Google Cloud Platform services.

Ansible is a tool for managing configurations that can also be used for IaC. It sets up infrastructure and automates jobs using simple YAML files that anyone can read.

**Pulumi:** This is an IaC tool that lets developers list and set up infrastructure using common computer languages like Go, Python, and JavaScript.

If you use their declarative programming languages (DSLs), Chef and Puppet, which are configuration management tools, you can change them to work with IaC.

### How to Set Up IaC: A Step-by-Step Guide

**Define Objectives:** Make sure you are clear on what your goals are and what parts of your infrastructure you want IaC to handle.

**Pick the Right Tool:** Pick an IaC tool that fits your needs and level of experience the best.

**Set up version control:** Make a Git project to store your IaC code and work on it with your team.

**Write Infrastructure Code:** Using the chosen IaC tool, write code to describe and set up your infrastructure resources.

**Test:** To make sure your system code is correct, use automated testing.

**Connect to CI/CD:** To make deployments more automatic, connect your IaC code to your CI/CD workflow.

**Follow best practices for security:** keep your IaC code and settings safe to keep private data safe.

**Monitor and Maintain:** To make sure your infrastructure is healthy and working well, set up regular maintenance and monitoring processes.

**grow and optimize:** As the needs of your business change, use IaC to grow and optimize your infrastructure to meet those needs.

Infrastructure as Code (IaC) is a powerful way for managing infrastructure that makes it easier to automate, be consistent, and grow. By thinking of infrastructure as software, businesses can speed up supply, cut down on mistakes, help teams work together better, and become more flexible overall. IaC can make it much easier for a company to handle and change its infrastructure in today's constantly changing IT world if it is set up using best practices and the right tools.

## 3.4 Handling Code Repositories and Version Control

In the software-driven world of today, software development teams must know how to handle code and keep track of versions. For cooperation, keeping track of changes, making sure code quality, and keeping the integrity of software projects, managing code repositories and putting in place version control systems are musts. The purpose of this piece is to explain why code repositories and version control are important, look at some best practices, and talk about the tools that are usually used for these tasks.

Why code repositories and version control are important

**Collaboration:** Code repositories let more than one worker work at the same time on a project. They give everyone on the team a central place to work together, add code, and plan their activities.

**Tracking Changes:** Version control systems (VCS) keep a complete record of all the changes that have been made to the software. Builders can see what changes were made, when they were made, and why they were made. This past is very helpful for finding bugs, doing audits, and seeing how the codebase has changed over time.

**Error Recovery:** Version control systems make it easy for developers to go back to earlier versions of the code if problems appear or changes are made without meaning to. This feature gives you a way to get back on track after making a mistake or having a problem.

**Quality of Code:** Version control supports good habits like code reviews that make code better. It lets developers give feedback, find bugs, and make sure that rules for writing code are followed.

**Branching and Parallel Development:** Version control systems let writers make branches so that work can be done at the same time on different projects. For example, you can use this to work on new features, bug fixes, or trials without affecting the main codebase.

**Collaborative Workflow:** Version control systems like GitFlow, GitHub Flow, and Feature Branching support different collaborative workflows that help teams handle complicated development processes more effectively.

**Continuous Integration and Deployment (CI/CD):** CI/CD pipelines let you test and release code changes automatically for CI/CD integration. This speeds up the release of software and makes code more reliable.

How to handle code repositories and version control in the best way

**Version Control Systems (VCS) should be used:** Pick a strong VCS like Perforce, Git, Mercurial, or Subversion (SVN). However, Git has become the standard because it is flexible, quick, and has strong splitting features.

**Set up a Repository Structure:** Make sure that your code repositories are set up in a way that is clear and uniform. For source code, documentation, and configuration files, use sensible directory names and follow the rules.

**Set up branching strategies:** Make clear plans for branching and joining. Pick a strategy that works with the way you create, like feature branching or GitFlow, and make sure everyone on the team knows about it.

**Commit Often:** Tell coders to commit changes to the code often, along with clear commit messages. It's easier to see and understand how the codebase has changed over time when changes happen often.

**Branch Naming Rules:** Make sure that the names of branches follow a pattern that makes sense in terms of what they are used for. Using consistent naming rules helps devs figure out what each branch is for.

**Code Reviews:** To keep the quality of your code high, set up a code review method. Code reviews are a way to find mistakes, share information, and make sure that code standards are being followed.

**Merge Conflicts:** Quickly handle merge conflicts. To keep conflicts to a minimum, update and merge your codebase often, and when they do happen, use merge tools or conflict resolution methods to get them fixed quickly.

**Automated Testing:** Make your version control method work with automated testing. Run tests before changes are made or pushed with pre-commit and pre-push hooks. This will make sure that the code meets quality standards.

**Releases and Tagging:** Tagging lets you mark certain versions of your software, especially ones that are ready for production. You can then go back to specific versions and keep a stable release history.

**instructions:** Keep detailed instructions in the place where you store your code. To make the codebase easier to understand and keep up to date, add README files, code comments, and inline instructions.

**Access Control:** Make sure that the right permissions and access controls are in place. Limit who can write to important branches and sources to stop changes that aren't supposed to be made.

**Keep integrating and deploying (CI/CD):** Connect version control to CI/CD pipelines to automatically test and release changes to code. This makes sure that code is always being checked and sent to production with as little human help as possible.

Tools that are often used for version control and code repositories

**Git:** Git is the most well-known method for sharing versions of files. It is famous for being fast, flexible, and able to branch in a lot of different ways. Sites like GitHub, GitLab, and Bitbucket all use Git.

**GitHub:** GitHub is a web-based tool based on Git that lets you host code, work together on it, review it, and keep track of issues. A lot of people use it for open-source projects and working together as a team.

**GitLab:** GitLab is a full DevOps tool that has a container registry, CI/CD pipelines, Git repository management, and more. It lets you choose between self-hosting and cloud-hosting.

**Bitbucket:** Bitbucket is an Atlassian service that hosts Git and Mercurial repositories. It has tools like CI/CD pipelines, code collaboration, and integration with Jira.

**Subversion (SVN):** SVN is a controlled version control system that handles versions in a more linear way than distributed systems like Git. It is still used by some businesses, especially ones with old codebases.

**Perforce:** Perforce is a version control system made to work with big files of code and data assets. It's used a lot in fields like games and space travel.

Managing code libraries and setting up version control systems are basic skills for making software today. These habits help people work together, write better code, keep track of changes, and fix mistakes, all of which eventually lead to the success of software projects. By using the right tools and following best practices, companies can speed up their development processes, make it easier for teams to work together, and make sure the stability and dependability of their codebase.

# Chapter 4

## Automated Testing in CI/CD

Continuous Integration/Continuous Delivery, or CI/CD, is now an important part of how software is developed today. It makes it possible to quickly and reliably build, test, and release software. Tests that are run automatically are an important part of a CI/CD workflow. This detailed guide will talk about why automated testing is important in CI/CD, what its benefits are, what the best practices are, and the different kinds of automatic tests that can be added to the pipeline.

What does CI/CD mean?

Software development techniques like Continuous Integration (CI) and Continuous Delivery (CD) are meant to make the process more efficient, quick, and reliable.

Continuous Integration (CI) means that changes to code made by many people are added to a shared folder several times a day. An automated build and automatic tests check each integration to find and fix integration problems early in the development cycle.

Continuous Delivery (CD), on the other hand, goes further than CI by putting code changes into a staging or production system automatically once they pass automated tests and other checks to make sure they are correct. This lets software be released quickly and reliably.

Why automated testing is important for CI/CD tests

1. Bugs are found early
   When changes are made to the code, automated tests are run right away. This helps find bugs and other problems early in the development process. Fixing problems later on will take less time and cost less money if they are found early.

2. Making sure the code is good
   Tests that are run automatically make sure that the code meets quality standards and acceptance factors. This makes sure that the code quality and consistency are good across the whole project.
3. Testing for Regression
   Code changes happen a lot in CI/CD processes. As a safety net, automated tests make sure that new changes don't cause regressions, which are unintended side effects that break current functionality.
4. Speeding up progress
   By automating testing jobs that are done over and over again, development teams can spend their time writing code instead of testing it by hand. This shortens the time it takes to get a product to market and speeds up the development process.
5. Feedback All the Time
   Automated test results give developers quick feedback, which lets them fix problems right away. This encourages a mindset of working together and always trying to get better.
6. Trust in the Releases

The goal of CD is to get code into production quickly and consistently. Automated tests are very important for making sure that changes to the code are ready for production, which boosts trust in the release process.

Why automated testing is good for CI/CD

1. Shorter time between projects
   Manual testing takes a lot of time, but automated testing gets rid of that need. This makes development cycles faster. Time-to-market is shortened because developers can make changes more quickly.
2. Less human error
   When checking by hand, mistakes can happen. Automated tests are reliable and can be run again and again, which makes it less likely that problems will be missed by accident.
3. More tests were done
   Unit tests, integration tests, and end-to-end tests can all be done automatically, so there is a lot of test coverage. This wide range of tests makes sure that different parts of the software are working properly.
4. Better working together
   Automated tests help everyone understand how the program works. This makes it easier for developers, testers, and other stakeholders

to work together, which improves dialogue and cuts down on misunderstandings.
5. **Constantly getting better**
Teams can keep improving the quality of their code and finding bugs early thanks to automatic testing's feedback loop. This lowers technical debt and maintenance costs.
6. **Sticking to it**
Code standards are enforced by automated tests, which also make sure that the software stays the same even as the team grows or changes.
7. **Quickly solving the problem**

When problems are found, automated tests give coders a lot of information about them, which helps them find and fix problems quickly.
Different Kinds of Computerized Tests

1. **Tests of individual units**
The main goal of unit tests is to check single pieces of code, like functions or methods, by themselves. These tools are quick and cover a lot of code at the lowest level.
2. **Tests of integration**
Integration tests make sure that the different parts or modules of the system work together correctly. They make sure that all of these parts work together the way it should.
3. **Tests of Function**
Functional tests check how well software works by putting it through specific use cases or needs. From the point of view of a customer, these tests see if the software works right.
4. **Tests from beginning to end (E2E)**
End-to-end tests act out how a user would interact with an app from beginning to end, usually through the user interface. They make sure that the whole system, all of its parts and services, works the way it should.
5. **Tests of Regression**
The goal of regression tests is to make sure that adding new code doesn't break or reverse the functionality that was already there. They are very important for keeping software stable as it changes.
6. **Tests of performance**
Performance tests look at how quickly, easily, and efficiently the program uses resources in different situations. Some common types are stress testing, load testing, and scaling testing.

7. Checks for security
   Security tests find holes and weak spots in the security of an application. This checks for common security problems like SQL injection, cross-site scripting (XSS), and problems with passwords.
8. Tests for accessibility
   According to accessibility standards like the Web Content Accessibility Guidelines (WCAG), accessibility tests make sure that the software can be used by people with disabilities.
9. Tests of usability

Usability tests check how easy it is to use and how good the user experience is. These tests help find problems with usefulness and places where things could be better.

How to do automated testing right in CI/CD

1. Make a plan before you start.
   Make a clear testing plan that tells you what to test, what kinds of tests to use, and when in the CI/CD process each test should run.
2. Set up automation early and often
   Test automatically from the start of the creation process. Run tests automatically as code is added to the folder to find problems quickly.
3. Keep track of versions
   Version control tools, like Git, can help you keep track of changes to code. This lets you keep track of changes, work together well, and go back to earlier versions if you need to.
4. Set up separate test environments
   Make sure that test settings can be replicated and kept separate. So, there is no interference between tests, and the answers are always the same.
5. Run test cases in parallel
   Parallelize the running of tests to cut down on the time it takes to run them, especially when you have a lot of tests to run. This can make the CI/CD process go a lot faster.
6. Monitoring all the time
   Keep an eye on the CI/CD workflow and test results all the time. Add tracking tools to find problems early and keep the pipeline running smoothly.
7. Keep up with a test pyramid
   It is recommended to have more unit tests than integration tests and more integration tests than end-to-end tests. Do not follow any other model. This improves the speed and range of the tests.

8. Make test data automatically
   Automate the process of making test data to make sure that tests are always the same. This is very important for end-to-end and interface tests.
9. Start reporting test results
   Make thorough test reports that include a lot of information about test fails, results, and trends. This helps teams find problems and decide which ones are most important.
10. Constantly getting better

Review and update automated tests often to keep up with changes to the codebase and needs. Tests stay useful and current by getting better all the time.

There are tools for automated testing in CI/CD.

1. TestNG and JUnit
   A lot of people use JUnit and TestNG to write and run unit and integration tests for Java tasks.
2. Test Pytest
   Unit, integration, and functional testing can all be done with Pytest, which is a famous testing framework for Python projects.
3. Iron Selenium
   Selenium is a strong tool for automating browser-based testing, which can include tests that run from beginning to end. It works with many programming systems.
4. A Cypress
   Cypress is an end-to-end testing tool for JavaScript that is known for being easy to use and showing a preview in the browser in real time while tests are running.
5. The Jenkins
   A lot of people use Jenkins, an open-source CI/CD server that lets you add automated tests to processes.
6. The Travis CI
   Travis CI is a CI/CD service that runs in the cloud and can be set up to run automatic tests when code changes.
7. The CircleI
   CircleCI is another CI/CD platform that runs in the cloud and lets you test and release code automatically.
8. CI/CD GitLab
   GitLab has an integrated CI/CD tool that supports automated testing out of the box. This makes it simple to set up pipelines.

## 9. TestRail and Jira

Jira and TestRail are two tools that can be added to the CI/CD process to help handle test cases and keep track of results.

Setting up automated testing in CI/CD

1. List the requirements for testing
   To begin, write down the testing needs for your project, including the types of tests that need to be done and the success factors.
2. Pick out the testing frameworks and tools
   Pick the right testing platforms and tools based on the technologies and needs of your project.
3. Make test plans
   Make sure that all of your application's features are covered by creating test cases and test sets for each type of test.
4. Add tests to the process flow
   You should add the automated tests to your CI/CD workflow. Setting up your CI/CD tool to run tests when code changes is usually what this means.
5. Keep an eye on and look over test results
   Check test results often and look them over to find problems and decide which ones are most important. For this process to go more smoothly, use tools for test reports.
6. Use and keep tests up to date
   Make sure that your automated tests are always up to date as the source changes. This means adding new tests for new features and changing the way old tests work when necessary.
7. Change the size as needed
   As your project gets bigger, you might want to think about scaling your testing system to keep up with the extra work and get feedback quickly.
8. Set up feedback that is continuous

By having everyone on the team help with testing, you can promote an atmosphere of constant feedback and improvement.

Problems and Things to Think About

1. Making sense of test data
   It can be hard to keep track of test results, especially for end-to-end and integration tests. It is necessary to have automated ways to create and manage test data.

2. Changes in the test environment
   False positives or negatives can happen when the test setting is different from the production environment. It is important to make sure that test settings are as much like production as possible.
3. Check for flakiness
   Because of outside factors or race conditions, automated studies may sometimes give mixed results. Test flakiness can be reduced by doing things like running the test again and reducing the number of external variables.
4. Using up resources
   A lot of computer resources may be needed to run a lot of tests at the same time. To keep pipeline efficiency high, it's important to use resources efficiently.
5. Check the cost of maintenance
   It takes ongoing work to keep a full set of automatic tests up to date. Test coverage and the cost of maintaining tests should be balanced by teams.
6. Test the Orchestra

It can be hard to plan and organize different kinds of tests, especially end-to-end tests. It can be helpful to have tools and systems that make test orchestration easier.

An important part of a good CI/CD pipeline is automated testing, which has many benefits that make the software development and release processes better. Development teams can make sure that their software is of high quality, reliable, and sent to production quickly and regularly by having a clear testing strategy, choosing the right tools and frameworks, and sticking to best practices. There are some problems with automatic testing in CI/CD, but the pros far outweigh the cons, making it an essential part of modern software development.

## 4.1 Types of Testing in CI/CD

Continuous Integration/Continuous Delivery (CI/CD) processes are an important part of modern software development because they help teams make high-quality software quickly and easily. Different kinds of tests are very important to the CI/CD process because they make sure that the software meets quality standards, works well, and doesn't have any major bugs. We will talk about the most popular types of testing in CI/CD, what they are used for, and how they fit into the software delivery lifecycle in this detailed guide.

1. Testing each unit
   Why: Unit testing is the first and most basic level of testing in CI/CD. In this method, testing single parts or pieces of code is the main goal. Each unit is usually a small function or method that works on its own.
   Important Points:
   Makes sure that each piece of code is right.
   Its goal is to find reasoning mistakes and functional problems.
   Since it is quick and effective, it can be used for regular execution in CI/CD pipelines.
   Usually written by the creators themselves.
   Often done automatically when the code changes.
   Good things:
   Finding bugs in code early on.
   Encourages code that is easy to update and is modular.
   Allows developers to get comments quickly.
   Sets the stage for documenting and understanding code.
2. Testing for integration
   Integration testing makes sure that different parts or pieces of the software work properly when put together and talk to each other. It makes sure that the combined system works the way it should.
   Important Points:
   Describes how the different parts of the software work together.
   Finds problems with connection, data flow, and compatibility.
   Can be done automatically and often.
   Could need test environments that are like the production system.
   Good things:
   Finds problems with merging early on.
   Proof that different parts of a system work together as a whole.
   Makes sure that data moves correctly between parts.
   boosts confidence in the system's general ability to work.
3. Testing how things work
   Functional testing checks how well the software works against clear requirements and specs. It checks that the program does what it's supposed to do and gives the right results.
   Important Points:
   focuses on functions that users can see and use.
   simulates how people would use the tools in real life.
   Checks the system's actions, inputs, and outputs.
   Do it by hand or automatically.
   Important for testing important ways that users work.
   Good things:

Makes sure the software meets the needs of both users and businesses.
Checks that important features do what they're supposed to do.
Helps find problems that affect the customer experience.
Gives an overall opinion on how well software works.

4. Testing from beginning to end

   End-to-end testing simulates how a user would deal with the whole piece of software from beginning to end. It makes sure that all the services and parts that are linked work together without any problems.

   **Important Points:**
   Checks that the software works in a number of different platforms.
   Usually looks at user interfaces and the paths that users take.
   Finds problems with system interaction, navigation, and data flow.
   Needs a test setting that is like real life.
   Usually done automatically, but it can use a lot of resources.

   **Good things:**
   Makes sure the program works with everything else.
   Checks important user cases for accuracy.
   Looks for problems with integrating systems.
   Gives people more faith that the application is ready for production.

5. Testing for Regression

   The goal of regression testing is to make sure that changes to new code don't create bugs or affect how old code works. It makes sure that the software's features that have already been tried continue to work right.

   **Important Points:**
   Tests functionality that has already been tried.
   After code changes or updates, this step is taken.
   Finds unexpected side effects and system regressions.
   It can be done automatically and is part of CI/CD processes.
   often includes a lot of different test cases.

   **Good things:**
   Stops known flaws from being introduced again.
   Protects against changes to the code that affect features that are already in use.
   Keeps software stable even as it changes.
   Validates the quality of the program all the time.

6. Testing for performance

   Performance testing checks how the software works in different situations, like when there are a lot of users, not enough resources, or extreme use cases. It makes sure that the software works the way it's supposed to.

**Important Points:**

This test includes stress testing, load testing, and scaling testing.

Response times, resource use, and system performance are all looked at.

Finds weaknesses and efficiency bottlenecks.

Often needs specific settings and tools.

Important for programs that have a lot of users or tasks that use a lot of resources.

**Good things:**

Finds problems with speed before they affect users.

Makes sure the software can handle the work that will be done with it.

Checks to see if the system meets speed standards.

Helps with plans for optimization and scalability.

7. Checking for security

   Why: Security testing checks how open the program is to attacks and threats of security. Malicious people could use the information to find flaws and holes in the system.

   **Important Points:**

   Attempts to find security holes, like SQL injection, cross-site scripting (XSS), and login problems.

   Checks how resistant the program is to common security threats.

   Needs special tools and knowledge for security tests.

   Offers suggestions for making security better.

   Important for keeping private information safe and following the rules.

   **Good things:**

   Keeps protection and data from being broken into.

   Stops people from taking advantage of known security holes.

   Shows a dedication to safety and following the rules.

   Builds trust with partners and users.

8. Testing for accessibility

   The goal of accessibility testing is to see how well the software can be used by people with disabilities. It makes sure that a wide range of people can use the program.

   **Important Points:**

   focuses on making sure that accessibility guidelines (like WCAG) are met.

   Looks at things like keyboard navigation, screen readers, and alternative text for pictures.

   Needs to be tested by people with disabilities or using special tools.

Makes sure that everyone is included and that the law is followed.
Good things:
makes it easier for a wider range of people to use.
Shows care for others and social duty.
Lowers the chance of being sued over mobility issues.
Makes the app more well-known and attracts more users.

9. Testing for usability

The goal of usability testing is to find out how easy it is to use software and how good the general user experience is. It gets comments from real users to find problems with how well it works.

Important Points:
uses real people to do jobs with the software.
get input on the design of the user interface, how easy it is to use, and how satisfied users are overall.
Usually done in a controlled setting or as part of UAT (user approval testing).
Needs a method based on feedback to make design changes.

Good things:
Finds problems with usability that coders might not see.
Boosts user happiness and the number of people who use it.
Makes the customer experience better overall.
Helps make choices about design and the user interface.

CI/CD pipelines need testing in order to deliver high-quality software that works reliably and meets user standards. Different types of testing are used to make sure that different parts of the software are correct, from small pieces of code to whole user trips. Adding a thorough testing plan to your CI/CD process will help you find and fix bugs faster, make sure the software meets speed and functionality needs, and improve security, usability, and accessibility. CI/CD pipelines that work well use a mix of these types of testing to make sure that the software they give is both reliable and full of features.

4.2 Integrating Testing Tools with CI/CD Pipelines

Continuous Integration/Continuous Delivery (CI/CD) has changed the way software is made by automating the processes of making, testing, and deploying software. Adding testing tools to CI/CD processes is a must if you want to get high-quality software out quickly. This complete guide will talk about why merging testing tools is important, what the benefits are, and how to do it in a way that works well.

Why integrating testing tools is important

1. Early notice of bugs
   Bugs and other problems can be found quickly by automated testing tools, often just minutes after code changes are committed to the file. This early discovery is very important for cutting down on the time and money needed to fix bugs.
2. Sticking to it
   Testing tools make sure that tests are run consistently and again and again. For example, people can make mistakes and be biased when they test things by hand, but automatic tests always give accurate results.
3. Quick Response
   Test tools let development teams get feedback quickly. This instant feedback loop lets developers fix problems right away, which speeds up the development process and the time it takes to get a product to market.
4. More tests were done
   Unit tests, integration tests, and end-to-end tests can all be automated to cover a lot of ground during testing. This wide range of tests makes sure that different parts of the software are working properly.
5. Testing for Regression
   For regression testing, automated testing tools are necessary to make sure that changes to new code don't cause bugs or regressions in functionality that was already there. This is especially important in agile development settings where code is updated often.
6. Testing for performance and scalability
   When performance testing tools are added to CI/CD processes, they can be used to test how well software works in different situations. This makes sure that the app can handle the expected amount of work and can grow as needed.
7. Checking for security
   There are special testing tools for security testing that help find holes and weak spots in an application's security. This is necessary to keep private data safe and in line with regulations.
8. Testing for usability and accessibility

Tools for checking usability and accessibility make sure that the software is easy for people to use and can be accessed by people with disabilities. The user experience and acceptance are both improved by these tools.

Pros of Putting Testing Tools Together

1. Shorter time between projects
   Iterating more quickly is possible for development teams when testing tasks are automated. This leads to shorter development cycles and faster time-to-market.
2. Better quality code
   By finding bugs and making sure that coding standards are followed, automated tests help keep the quality of code good. This lowers the risk of releasing bad software and technical debt.
3. Less work done by hand
   Automation gets rid of the need for manual testing, so developers can focus on writing code and testers can work on more difficult and exploratory testing jobs.
4. Feedback All the Time
   Testing tools give development teams feedback all the time, which encourages them to keep improving and work together as a team.
5. Being consistent and dependable
   Automated tests make sure that testing methods are consistent and can be used again and again. This makes results more reliable and lowers the chance of mistakes made by humans.
6. Releases with more confidence

With automatic testing, development teams can be more sure that changes to the code are ready for production, which lowers the chance of problems after the release.

How to Easily Add Testing Tools to Your System

1. Pick the Apps You Need for Testing
   Pick testing tools that work with the technologies your project uses, the tests you need to run, and your budget. Unit testing, integration testing, speed testing, security testing, and more are all popular types of testing tools.
2. Setting up version control and a repository
   Use a version control system like Git to keep track of your software. A file that keeps track of versions should hold all changes to code and test scripts.
3. Set up pipelines for CI/CD
   Use tools like Jenkins, Travis CI, CircleCI, GitLab CI/CD, and others to set up CI/CD workflows. With these tools, automation is easier, and you can set up and run tests at different points in the process.
4. Put testing tools together
   Add the testing steps or scripts that go with your chosen testing tools

to your CI/CD processes. Usually, this means setting up your CI/CD tool so that tests run immediately whenever the code changes.

5. Explain how you will test

   Make sure your project's testing plans are clear. Pick out the types of tests that should be automatic and the ones that should still be done by hand. Set rules for the process about when and where each type of test should run.

6. Make test execution automatic

   Use the right testing platforms and tools to write and automate your tests. Make sure your tests are reliable, can be updated, and give you thorough test results.

7. Run test cases in parallel

   Tests should be run in parallel, especially if you have a big test suite. Your CI/CD process can go a lot faster if you run tests at the same time.

8. Keep an eye on and look over test results

   Set up ways to keep an eye on test results and report them. Keep an eye on your CI/CD pipeline's health and look at test results to find problems and patterns.

9. Managing the test environment

   Keep test environments that are separate, can be copied, and are very similar to the production system. This stops problems with the setting and makes sure that testing is always the same.

10. Constantly getting better

    Review and update your automated tests often to keep up with changes to the codebase and needs. Making improvements all the time makes sure that your tests are still useful and important.

11. Safety and following the rules

    There are special tools that can find flaws and holes in security that should be used for testing. Make sure that your program follows the rules for privacy and security.

12. Testing for usability and accessibility

    Use usability and accessibility testing tools to see how accessible and easy the software is for people to use. Get opinions from people who use the site with disabilities or special tools.

13. Working together and talking to each other

    Get the production, testing, and operations teams to work together more. Encourage open conversation, sharing of test results, and working together to solve problems.

14. Resource management and the ability to grow

Improve the scalability and resource efficiency of your CI/CD workflow. Make sure that the right tools are used to keep the pipeline running smoothly.

Problems and Things to Think About

1. Making sense of test data
   It can be hard to keep track of test results, especially for end-to-end and integration tests. To make sure uniformity, use automated tools to create and organize test data.
2. Changes in the test environment
   False positives or negatives can happen when the test setting is different from the production environment. It's important to make sure that test settings are a lot like production.
3. Check for flakiness
   Because of outside factors or race conditions, automated studies may sometimes give mixed results. Test flakiness can be reduced by doing things like running the test again and reducing the number of external variables.
4. Check the cost of maintenance
   It takes ongoing work to keep a full set of automatic tests up to date. Test coverage and the cost of maintaining tests should be balanced by teams.
5. Putting together tests

It can be hard to plan and organize different kinds of tests, especially end-to-end tests. It can be helpful to have tools and systems that make test orchestration easier.

Adding testing tools to CI/CD pipelines is necessary to quickly and reliably produce high-quality software. Development teams can speed up development processes, improve code quality, and cut down on manual work by choosing the right testing tools, making clear testing strategies, and automating test execution. Even though it can be hard, integrating testing tools has a lot of benefits that make it an important part of current software development and CI/CD processes.

4.3 Ensuring Test Coverage and Quality

Making sure that all tests are covered and that high-quality testing methods are kept up are important parts of making software that works well. It is important to have good testing plans in place before putting out software that you can trust. This complete guide will talk about how important test coverage and quality are, the best ways to get them, and the benefits they provide.

## How to Understand Quality and Test Coverage

### Coverage of Tests

What is test coverage? It tells you how much of your codebase your tests use. It solves the question, "How deeply have my tests looked into my code?" A percentage is often used to show test coverage, which is the number of code lines, functions, or branches that have been run by your tests.

### Test the Quality

"Test quality" refers to how well and consistently your tests work. High-quality tests give developers useful input, give them reliable results, and find bugs correctly. They also follow best practices and standards for maintainability.

### Why test coverage is important

1. **Looking for bugs**
   More flaws are likely to be found by tests with high coverage. This makes sure that bugs are found and fixed before they get to production. Fixing problems after the release is easier and costs less because of this.

2. **Trust in the Code**
   A high test coverage rate makes people trust the software. It lets writers, testers, and other important people know that the software has been carefully checked out and is less likely to have any bugs that were missed.

3. **Stopping Regression**
   Regressions happen when changes to the code have unintended side effects that break current functionality. Comprehensive test coverage helps stop regressions. Regression prevention is very important in rapid development because code changes so often.

4. **Making sure the quality**

Full test coverage improves the quality of software by making sure that the code meets customer needs, follows the requirements, and works as expected.

### Best Practices for Making Sure Quality and Test Coverage

1. **Make sure the testing goals are clear.**
   Set clear goals and objectives for each step of testing. Find out what parts of the software need to be tried and what testing methods will work best.

2. Put together a test pyramid
   It is recommended to have more unit tests than integration tests and more integration tests than end-to-end tests. Do not follow any other model. This structure makes the best use of test coverage and processing speed.
3. Test automatically
   Test as many things as you can automatically. Automated tests are reliable, can be run over and over, and can be done often. They are very useful for continuous integration and checking for bugs.
4. Make Critical Path Testing a Top Priority
   Find the most important user flows or key paths in your app and test those first. A lot of tests should be run on these paths because they often show the most important features.
5. Use reviews of the code
   Get your friends to help you review the code to make sure that changes are properly tested.
   Code reviews can help you figure out which parts of the code need more testing.
6. Do tests to find out more.
   Exploratory testing should be done in addition to automatic testing to find problems that automated test cases might not cover. Exploratory testing depends on how creative and knowledgeable the testers are in the field.
7. Use tools that check for code coverage
   Use code coverage tools to get a good picture of how well your tests are covered. These tools give you data and visuals that can help you find code that isn't being covered.
8. Keep up with a suite of regression tests
   Make and keep up with a set of bug tests that cover the most important features. Run these tests often to make sure that changes to new code don't cause regressions.
9. Keep an eye on test results
   Keep an eye on the test results and keep in touch with the authors. Check into and fix test failures right away to make sure they aren't false positives and that problems are solved.
10. Start reporting test results
    Make thorough test reports that include a lot of information about test fails, results, and trends. Test reports help find problems and put them in order of importance.
11. Constantly getting better
    Review and update your test suite often to keep up with changes to

the codebase and needs. Making improvements all the time makes sure that your tests are still useful and important.
12. Get people to work together
Encourage the teams that work on programming, testing, and operations to work together. Collaboration and good communication can help find testing holes and make sure that all tests are covered.
13. Make sure you can manage test data
Effectively manage test data to make sure that tests can be run regularly and with the right data. Create and keep track of test data generation and maintenance options.
14. Test in different places

Test your software in a number of settings that are as close as possible to real life. This helps make sure that your tests are strong and catch problems that are unique to the setting.

The Advantages of Quality and Full Test Coverage

1. Fewer mistakes in production
A lot of testing helps find bugs early on in the development process, which lowers the number of bugs that get into production.
2. Better quality code
Good tests make sure that developers follow coding standards and write code that is clean, modular, and easy to manage.
3. Shorter time between projects
Shorter development cycles and faster time-to-market are both benefits of good testing methods, such as automation and preventing regression.
4. More self-assurance
Full test coverage builds trust in the software's dependability and accuracy, which makes users and stakeholders more likely to trust it.
5. Lower costs for repairs
Lower maintenance costs over the lifetime of the software are achieved by finding bugs early and stopping regressions before they happen.
6. Better working together
Good testing practices allow the development and testing teams to work together, which improves communication and understanding.
7. A better experience for users
Good testing makes sure that the software meets the needs of users, which leads to a good experience for users and higher customer happiness.

8. Security and following the rules

Utilizing good testing methods helps make sure that regulations are followed and finds security holes.

Problems and Things to Think About

1. **Finding the Right Test Coverage**
   It's not always possible to get 100% test coverage. It is very important to find the right balance between coverage and growth time and resources.
2. **Keeping test suites up to date**
   It can be hard to keep up with large test sets, which can lead to test code that is hard to understand and prone to mistakes.
3. **Taking care of test data**
   Keeping track of test results can be hard, especially in systems that are complicated. It is very important to use good test data management systems.
4. **Finding holes in the tests**
   It can be hard to find parts of the script that aren't covered or don't have good enough tests. Reviewing the code often and working together can help close these gaps.
5. **Changes in the test environment**

False positives or negatives can happen when the test setting is different from the production environment. It's important to make sure that test settings are a lot like production.

For stable and high-quality software to be delivered, tests must cover a lot of ground and be of high quality. These goals can be reached by development teams following best practices, using automation, putting important features first, and encouraging teamwork. Fewer bugs in production, better code quality, shorter development cycles, and better user experiences are some of the perks. Even though it can be hard, investing in good testing methods is necessary to make sure that software fits users' needs and works reliably.

4.4 Test Automation Strategies

Test automation is an important part of modern software development because it helps teams be more productive, make sure that all tests are run, and get high-quality software out faster. But for test automation to work, it needs to be carefully planned out and have a clear strategy. We will talk about different test automation methods, best practices, and things to think about in this in-depth guide to help you automate your software testing process effectively.

Why test automation is important

1. Speed and ease of use
   Automated tests can be run quickly and over and over again, which cuts down on testing time and lets development teams get feedback more quickly.
2. Being consistent and dependable
   The risk of human mistake in testing is lower when tests are automated because the results are always the same.
3. More tests were done
   Automation lets you do a lot of tests, like unit tests, integration tests, and end-to-end tests, which make sure that the software is fully tested.
4. Testing for Regression
   Regression testing needs automated tests to make sure that changes to the code don't introduce new bugs or break current features.
5. Support for continuous integration and delivery (CI/CD)

Automation works well with CI/CD pipelines because it lets tests run automatically when code changes. This encourages continuous delivery and release.

Strategies for automating tests

1. Make your goals clear.
   Set clear goals for test automation as a first step. Know what the goals are, what the expected results will be, and how far technology will go. Figure out which types of tests (like unit, integration, end-to-end, and speed tests) should be automated and which ones should still be done by hand.
2. Picking the Test
   Not all tests can be done automatically. Set the order of tests based on things like how often they are run, how important they are, and how stable the system is. Start with tests that have a big effect and cover a lot of ground.
3. Choosing an automation framework
   Pick the right automation system or tool for your project based on the technologies it uses, the tests it needs, and the skills of your team. Selenium, Appium, JUnit, TestNG, and many others are well-known automation tools.

4. Looking after test data
   Take good care of test data so that automated tests can run regularly with the right data. As needed, put in place solutions for making and keeping test results.
5. Managing the test environment
   Keep test environments that are separate, can be copied, and are very similar to the production system. For testing to be reliable, the test setting must be the same as the production environment.
6. Making a test script
   Make sure your test scripts are clear, modular, and easy to manage. Follow best practices for coding, like reusing code, fixing errors, and writing clear instructions. Make tests that are simple to understand and keep up to date.
7. Running tests in parallel
   Parallelize the running of tests to cut down on the time it takes to run tests. Running tests at the same time makes the best use of resources and speeds up the testing process.
8. Integration with Continuous Integration (CI)
   You should add test automation to your CI/CD workflow. Set up your CI server (like Jenkins, Travis CI, or CircleCI) so that when you change code, it will automatically run tests.
9. Reporting tests and getting feedback
   Set up strong ways to report tests so that you can record and analyze test data. Use test reporting tools and platforms to let the development and testing teams know what you think.
10. Check up on maintenance
    Automating tests is an ongoing project. Review and update your automated tests often to keep up with changes in the codebase, needs, and technologies. Make plans for keeping your test suite up to date.
11. Making versions of test data and environments
    Along with your software, version control test data and test environments. This makes sure that for each version of your app, the right test data and settings are used.
12. Feedback and teamwork all the time
    Encourage team members to give and receive comments all the time and work together. Ask testers, coders, and other important people to take an active role in the testing process.
13. Ability to grow

Plan for scalability by making sure that your automation system can handle more tests and test environments as they come up. For big projects, think about using spread testing methods.

The best ways to make test automation work

1. Getting involved early
   Early on in the development process, testers and automation engineers should be brought in to define test automation needs and find automation possibilities.
2. Keep your codebase clean
   Make sure the software for your app is clean, modular, and follows best practices. It's easier to test and execute code that is well organized.
3. Separate the test
   Make sure that each test is separate from the others. If you don't want one test failure to affect other tests, don't make them depend on each other.
4. Keep track of versions
   Git is a version control system that can be used to store test files and code for automating tasks. This makes it easier to work together, keep track of versions, and collaborate.
5. Monitoring all the time
   Always keep an eye on the health of your test automation suite. Set up alerts for when a test fails, and quickly look into and fix any problems that are found.
6. Make sure tests are quick and stable
   Fast, stable, and accurate writing tests should be given the most weight. Flaky tests or tests that take a long time to run can make your software less useful.
7. Proof of ownership
   Keep detailed records of your automated tests, such as descriptions of test cases, standards for prerequisites, and test data needs.
8. Regular checks of the code
   Review the code for test scripts and automation scripts to find problems and fix them, make sure it follows coding standards, and make it easier to manage.
9. Plan to test data
   Set up a plan for how to handle test results. To do this, you might need to use tools for creating data, hide private data, and keep data snapshots.
10. Learning all the time

Keep up with the newest platforms, tools, and best practices for automation. Encourage your team to learn new things and share what they already know.

Problems and Things to Think About

1. The first investment
   Setting up test automation takes some time and money at the beginning, because you have to
   choose an automation tool, build a structure, and write scripts.
2. Costs of maintenance
   Keeping up with automatic tests can take a lot of time. As the app changes, the tests need to be updated to match the new features and requirements.
3. Negatives or false positives
   There are many reasons why automated tests might give false positives or negatives, such as test flaws or problems with the surroundings. There needs to be a way to cut down on fake results.
4. Trained and skilled
   To automate tests, you need engineers who are skilled and know how to use automation frameworks, write code, and follow testing concepts. It is important to put money into training and skill growth.
5. Taking care of test data
   Keeping track of test results can be hard, especially when dealing with complicated situations. It is very important to use good test data management systems.
6. Compatibility with Tools

Make sure that the automation tools you choose can work with the technologies you already have and can handle the types of tests you want to automate.

Test automation that works well is an important part of current software development because it speeds up the testing process, makes it more reliable, and covers more tests. You can use automation to speed up development cycles and make sure high-quality software is delivered by sticking to clear test automation strategies and best practices and being aware of the challenges. Keep in mind that test automation is an ongoing process that needs to be constantly supervised, maintained, and worked on by the whole team in order to reach its full potential.

# Chapter 5

## Continuous Integration in the Cloud

Continuous Integration (CI) is an important part of current software development that aims to make software delivery faster, better, and more efficient. CI in the cloud has become an important part of the software development process as more businesses use cloud computing. This piece talks about Continuous Integration in the Cloud, including what it is, how it works, and what tools and services are needed to make it work.

1. What Continuous Integration Means

1.1. What does "continuous integration" mean?
As part of continuous integration, code changes made by multiple coders are constantly merged into a shared repository. This is followed by an automated build and testing process. The main goal is to find and fix integration problems as early as possible in the development process. This will make sure that the software stays uniform and works as it changes.
1.2. The main ideas behind CI

1. **Frequent Code Commits:** Developers make small changes to the public repository several times a day. This lowers the chance of code that doesn't work with other code and problems with integration.
2. **Automatic Builds:** Continuous integration (CI) tools compile the code, make artifacts, and make a version of the software that can be deployed.
3. **Automated Testing:** Faults and regressions are found by running a set of automated tests that includes unit, integration, and functional tests.

4. **Instant Feedback:** When developers make changes to code, they get feedback right away, which helps them fix problems quickly.
5. **Deployment Readiness:** Continuous Integration (CI) makes sure that the code can always be deployed, which lets updates happen quickly and reliably.

## II. CI and the cloud
### 2.1. Infrastructure for the cloud

1. **Scalability:** When build and test workloads go up, cloud services can easily add more resources to handle them.
2. **Cost-effectiveness:** Pay-as-you-go pricing models let you use resources in a way that saves you money.
3. **Geographical Distribution:** Cloud companies have data centers in many places, which lowers latency and makes it easier for development teams that work in different places to access resources.

### 2.2. Pros of CI in the Cloud

1. **Availability of Resources:** The cloud provides resources on demand, which means that CI builds and tests are not limited by hardware.
2. **Collaboration:** Cloud-based files and continuous integration (CI) tools make it easy for developers in different places to work together.
3. **Flexibility:** A lot of different computer languages, frameworks, and tools can be used with cloud-based CI.
4. **Integration with Cloud Services:** CI tools can use other cloud services, like Kubernetes for container management and AWS Lambda for serverless computing, to make their features better.

## III. Setting up CI in the cloud
### 3.1. Setting up a CI Space

1. **Choosing a CI Service:** AWS CodePipeline, Azure DevOps, and Google Cloud Build are all CI/CD services that cloud companies offer. These services make setting up CI easier.
2. **Repository Management:** Use version control systems that are stored in the cloud, like Git repositories, or connect to popular platforms, like GitHub and Bitbucket.
3. **CI setup:** The CI process can be automated by setting up setup files (like YAML) with build scripts, test suites, and deployment pipelines.

### 3.2. CI/CD Chains

1. **Define the pipeline:** Make CI/CD pipelines that list the steps, actions, and variables needed to develop, test, and release software.
2. **Automated Triggers:** Set up pipelines to run when code is committed to make sure continuous integration.
3. **Parallelization:** Use cloud resources to run test and build jobs at the same time, which speeds up the build process.
4. **Artifact Management:** Use cloud-based artifact repositories, like Amazon S3 and Google Cloud Storage, to store and work with build files.

### 3.3. Isolation from the environment

1. Keep the build and test settings separate by using containers or serverless functions. This will make sure that everything is the same and can be repeated.
2. **Disposable Environments:** For each CI build, make an ephemeral environment so that earlier builds don't contaminate it.

## IV. The Best Ways to Use CI in the Cloud
### 4.1. Exams Done Automatically

1. **Full Test Suite:** Make a strong set of automatic tests that include unit tests, integration tests, and end-to-end tests.
2. **Test Coverage:** Aim for high test coverage to lower the chance that bugs won't be found.
3. **Testing in Parallel:** Use cloud tools to run tests at the same time, which speeds up feedback.

### 4.2. Infrastructure as Code

1. Define infrastructure using IaC tools like AWS CloudFormation or Terraform to make sure settings are consistent and can be used again and again.
2. Automate infrastructure provisioning by adding IaC to CI/CD workflows.

### 4.3. Checking for security

1. Add security screening tools to CI to find security holes and holes in the code early in the development process.
2. **Container Security:** To check how safe container pictures are, use tools that scan containers.

### 4.4. Watching and keeping records

1. Add tracking and logging to applications to find problems in production and after deployment.
2. Connect monitoring tools to CI/CD pipelines to make sure that changes to the code don't cause speed problems.

## V. Problems and Things to Think About
### 5.1. Privacy and Compliance with Data

1. When you store and handle data in the cloud, think about the rules about data privacy.
2. To keep private data safe, use encryption and access controls.

### 5.2. Being locked into one vendor

1. Think about the provider lock-in that might come with cloud-based CI/CD services and pick technologies that can be moved around.

### 5.3. Keeping track of costs

1. Keep an eye on and improve how cloud resources are used to avoid the hidden costs that come with overprovisioning.

## VI. Cloud-based CI tools and services
### 6.1. CodePipeline for AWS

1. Amazon's CI/CD service for making apps, testing them, and putting them online.
2. It works with other AWS services, such as AWS CodeBuild and AWS CodeDeploy.

### 6.2. Develop and deploy apps in Azure

Microsoft offers a full CI/CD tool that works with Git repositories and many different programming languages and frameworks.

### 6.3. Build on Google Cloud

The CI/CD tool from Google automates the build and test processes and works with resources and repositories in Google Cloud.

### 6.4. The Jenkins

A free automation server that can be set up in the cloud and customized to work with different CI/CD processes.

Continuous Integration in the Cloud is a revolutionary way to build software that takes advantage of the cloud's resources, freedom, and ability to grow. Companies that use CI in the cloud can speed up their development processes, make it easier for people to work together, and make better software products. For implementation to go well, you need to follow best practices, combine security and tracking, and pick the right tools and services. CI in the cloud will stay an important part of modern software development, even as technology changes. It will drive innovation and efficiency in the industry.

### 5.1 Setting Up CI Environments

Setting up CI environments is a key part of putting Continuous Integration (CI) and Continuous Deployment (CD) pipelines into action. CI is an important part of current software development. CI environments make it possible for build, test, and release processes to be automated. This lets teams deliver software more quickly and better. This post will talk about the most important parts of setting up CI environments, such as best practices, things to think about, and the tools and methods that work best for this process.

1. Learning About CI Environments

1.1. What does a CI Stand for?

A CI environment is a controlled and automated workspace where changes to code are made, tried, and approved to make sure the quality and functionality of the software. These environments are made to be as much like production as possible while still being separate enough to keep disagreements and problems from happening during the CI process.

1.2. Important Parts of a CI Environment

1. **Source Code Repository:** The source code for the project is kept in a version control system like Git.
2. **Build Server:** The build server is in charge of compiling the code, handling dependencies, and making files that can be run.

3. **Infrastructure for Testing:** CI systems have infrastructure for running different types of tests, like unit, integration, and end-to-end tests.
4. **Artifact Repository:** This is where the binaries and packages that are made during the build process are kept so that they can be used later.
5. **Mechanisms for Isolation:** Continuous integration (CI) setups should have ways to keep one build or test from affecting other builds or tests. Virtualization, containerization, and serverless tools can all be used to do this.

## II. The Best Ways to Set Up CI Environments

### 2.1. Infrastructure as Code

Use Infrastructure as Code (IaC) tools like Terraform, AWS CloudFormation, or Ansible to set up CI setups. This is one of the best ways to do it. IaC lets you describe and set up your infrastructure using code, which makes sure that everything is the same in all environments.

Why IaC is useful in CI environments:

1. **Version Control:** Infrastructure descriptions are kept in code repositories, which lets you track versions and changes.
2. **Reproducibility:** IaC makes sure that CI environments can be duplicated exactly as needed, which lowers the risk of problems that are caused by the environment.
3. **Collaboration:** Teams can work together to make changes to infrastructure and then use normal code review methods to look over them.

### 2.2. Isolation from the environment

1. **Virtual Machines (VMs):** Using VMs to make different environments for each test or build gives you strong isolation, but it can use a lot of resources.
2. **Containers:** Technologies for containerization, such as Docker, offer light isolation, which makes it easier to handle and grow CI environments.
3. **Serverless:** Platforms for serverless computing, such as AWS Lambda, let you run code in separate, event-driven settings, which lowers the cost of operations.

### 2.3. It can grow

CI systems should be able to handle different amounts of work. Cloud service companies let you use auto-scaling, which lets you assign resources based on demand. This makes sure that your CI process works well even when development is busy.

## 2.4 Taking Care of Artifacts

In CI environments, it's very important to handle artifacts well. It is important to store artifacts like build results and dependencies in a safe and organized way. You could use cloud-based storage services like Amazon S3 or Google Cloud Storage, or you could use artifact libraries like JFrog Artifactory or Sonatype Nexus.

Artifact management has these pros:

1. **Reproducibility:** Keeping build files safe lets you confidently repeat previous builds and deployments.
2. **Dependency Management:** Make it easy for teams and projects to share and handle dependencies.
3. **Security:** Access controls and vulnerability checking are common security features that are built into artifact repositories.

## 2.5. Testing Without Humans

CI environments should make it easy to perform testing at different levels, such as end-to-end, unit, and integration. You can set up tools like Jenkins, Travis CI, and CircleCI to run test suites automatically when code changes. This lets workers get feedback quickly.

Pros of using automated testing in CI environments:

1. **Early Issue Discovery:** Bugs and regressions are found early in the development process by automated tests.
2. **Consistency:** Built-in tests make sure that the software works the same way in all settings.
3. **Faster Feedback:** Running tests quickly speeds up the development process, which lets changes happen more quickly.

## III. Things to think about when setting up CI environments

### 3.1. Keeping track of costs

Cloud services can be used on a large or small scale, but they cost money. To avoid surprise costs, it's important to keep an eye on and improve how resources are used. Setting up budget alerts, tagging resources, and reviewing usage reports on a regular basis can all help you control costs better.

### 3.2. Privacy and Compliance with Data

When setting up CI environments, especially if they will be working with private data, think about data privacy laws. Make sure that data is kept and processed safely, and use encryption and access controls as needed to follow the laws and rules that apply.

### 3.3. Management of configurations

It is very important to keep settings the same across CI environments. To organize and standardize how environments are set up, use configuration management tools such as Puppet, Chef, or Ansible. As a result, configuration drift is lessened, and settings stay the same over time.

### 3.4. Connecting to CI/CD Pipelines

CI environments and CI/CD processes should work together without any problems. Make sure that the way you set up your CI environment lets good builds be automatically sent to staging or production environments. Some well-known CI/CD tools, like Azure DevOps, Jenkins, and GitLab CI/CD, have features that make this connection easier.

## IV. Tools and Technologies for Setting Up a CI Environment

### 4.1. Docker

Docker is a well-known containerization platform that makes it easier to separate environments and bundles dependencies and apps together. For complex CI processes, Docker Compose can be used to set up environments with multiple containers.

### 4.2. Containers

Kubernetes is an orchestration tool that can handle rolling out containers and making them

bigger or smaller in a CI environment. It comes with powerful tools for managing program lifecycles and automating CI/CD workflows.

### 4.3. Lambda from AWS

As a serverless computing tool, AWS Lambda lets you run code without having to worry about managing servers. On its own, it can be used for event-driven CI jobs like building artifacts or running tests.

### 4.4. The Jenkins

A lot of people use Jenkins, an open-source CI/CD automation system. It works with a lot of

plugins and can be set up to set up and handle CI environments well.

In order to use Continuous Integration for software development, you need to set up CI servers. It is recommended that companies follow best practices like Infrastructure as Code, environment isolation, scalability, and automatic testing to make their CI processes more efficient and boost the quality of their software. CI environments are also efficient and legal when things like cost management, data privacy, and configuration management are taken into account. The development team should pick tools and technologies that fit their needs and goals. This will help them release software faster, more reliably, and of higher quality.

## 5.2 Triggering Builds and Tests

A key part of setting up a good Continuous Integration (CI) pipeline is setting off builds and tests. It involves automating the process of building and testing software every time changes are made to a version control system. This makes sure that coders get feedback quickly and keeps the quality of the code high. This article will talk about different approaches, best practices, and tools that can be used to successfully run builds and tests in a CI environment.

1. Why automated triggers are important

1.1. How do I use automated triggers in CI?

In CI, automated triggers are the parts and steps that start build and test jobs automatically when certain things happen, usually when code is committed or other changes are made to the source code file. These triggers are very important for continuous integration because they let you find integration problems, bugs, and regressions right away.

1.2. Why automated triggers are helpful

1. **Quick Feedback:** Automated triggers give workers feedback right away, which helps them find and fix problems early in the development process.
2. **Consistency:** Automated triggers make sure that every change to the code goes through the same build and test steps. This keeps the workflow reliable and consistent.
3. **Scalability:** As development teams and codebases grow, automatic triggers make it easy for CI processes to be scaled up to handle more work.

II. Plans for beginning builds and tests

2.1. Triggers Based on Events

1. **Code Commits:** This is the most common trigger, and it starts a build and test job every time change is made to the repository.
2. **Pull Requests:** Making sure that suggested changes are looked at before merging is done by starting builds and tests when pull requests are opened or updated.
3. **Making a Branch:** Starting CI jobs when new branches are made lets feature branches be tested separately.

## 2.2. Periodic Triggers

Periodic triggers set up tests and builds to happen at set times. Even though they aren't as quick to respond as event-driven triggers, they can help make sure that jobs that take a lot of time or resources are run on a regular basis.

## 2.3. Triggers by Hand

A user, usually a developer or CI/CD administrator, sets off a manual trigger when certain situations call for manual action. This can help you run tests on the spot, send to staging environments, or do other tasks that aren't automated.

## III. The best ways to start builds and tests

### 3.1. Make as many tasks as you can automatic

Automation is what CI is all about, so try to automate events as much as you can. Event-driven events, like code commits and pull requests, should be the main ways that CI processes start. Cut down on the number of manual triggers you use to keep your CI workflow consistent and lower the chance of human error.

### 3.2 .Full Test Suites

To make sure the quality of your code is strong, you should make test sets that include unit tests, integration tests, and end-to-end tests. Set up automatic triggers to run the whole suite every time the code changes. This will help you find bugs and regressions quickly.

### 3.3. The use of parallelism

Use parallelization to get the most out of running build and test jobs. Creating smaller, parallelizable units within test suites can greatly shorten the time it takes to run tests, letting devs get feedback more quickly. A lot of CI systems and tools can run multiple tasks at the same time right out of the box.

### 3.4. Being alone

For each build and test job, keep the CI setup clean and separate. To make sure that one job doesn't get in the way of others, use virtualization or containerization tools like Docker. This lowers the chance of problems and makes it easier to repeat builds and tests.

### 3.5. Alerts and notifications

Set up ways for development teams to be notified about the state and results of CI builds and tests. Developers are quickly notified of any problems through email alerts, chat apps (like Slack), and integration with teamwork programs.

### 3.6. The Levels of Test Coverage

Set test coverage limits to make sure that standards for minimum code coverage are met. If code changes don't meet these standards, automated triggers can stop them from being merged. This makes sure that new code additions keep up with test coverage.

## IV. Services and tools for starting CI builds and tests

### 4.1. The Jenkins

Jenkins is a popular open-source automation service that can be set off by code commits, pull requests, and regular schedules, among other things. Jenkins has a lot of plugin support, which lets it work with warning services and version control systems.

### 4.2. Travis CM

Travis CI is a CI/CD tool in the cloud that is made for GitHub repositories. It makes setting up CI for GitHub projects easier by immediately running builds and tests when code is pushed or pulled.

### 4.3. Make a circleCI

CircleCI is a CI/CD platform that lets you choose how to start things in different ways. It lets you set event-driven triggers for things like code changes, pull requests, and branch creation. You can also set manual and periodic triggers.

### 4.4. The GitLab CI/CD tool

GitLab CI/CD works nicely with GitLab files and has CI/CD features built right in. You can set human or automatic triggers for things like code commits and pull requests, as well as event-driven triggers.

### 4.5. Actions on GitHub

GitHub Actions is a CI/CD service that is built right into GitHub projects. It makes it easy for GitHub users by letting them set off events for code changes, pull requests, and other GitHub events.

## V. Problems and Things to Think About

### 5.1. Overhead and Use of Resources

A lot of automated triggers can use up a lot of resources, especially on big tasks. It's important to carefully control how resources are used, and cloud-based CI/CD services may offer ways to scale up resources as needed.

### 5.2. Negatives and false positives

Too many automatic triggers can cause false positives (like build failures due to changes that aren't code) or false negatives (like tests passing even though there are problems with the code). These problems can be fixed by fine-tuning the trigger conditions and adding clever test selection.

### 5.3. Tiredness from notifications

Notification burnout can happen on development teams when they get too many of them. Set up alerts wisely to give team members the information they need without sending too many of them.

One important part of Continuous Integration is setting off builds and tests. This lets problems in software development be found and fixed quickly. For a streamlined and successful CI/CD pipeline, use automated triggers, full test suites, parallelization, isolation, and good notifications. By using the right tools and services and following best practices, development teams can make high-quality software quickly and reliably, which improves the whole software development process.

## 5.3 Handling Build Artifacts

A key part of the Continuous Integration (CI) process is dealing with build data. Build artifacts are what you get when you compile, test, and package changes to code. They are very important for making sure that software deployments are reliable and can be done again and again. This article will talk about why it's important to handle build artifacts correctly, the best ways to do that, and how to make sure they fit easily into the CI/CD (Continuous Integration/Continuous Deployment) workflow.

### 1. Getting to Know Build Artifacts

#### 1.1. What Are Stuff You Can Build?

The files that are made during the build process are called build artifacts. They have libraries, instructions, configuration files, compiled binaries, and any other files that are needed to run the software. The CI pipeline's work can be seen and touched in these artifacts, which are then used for more testing, release, and distribution.

#### 1.2. Different Kinds of Building Tools

1. **Binary Executables:** These are the completed and ready-to-run files for the software program.
2. **Libraries:** The app needs shared or static libraries to work.
3. **instructions:** This includes user guides, API instructions, and other files that explain things.
4. **setup Files:** These are files that hold the application's setup settings.
5. **Deployment Packages:** These are archives or packages that can be used to send to different environments, like Docker images, containers, and deployment scripts.

### II. Why it's Important to Handle Build Artifacts

#### 2.1. The ability to repeat

It is necessary to have build artifacts in order to recreate the same software environment at different points in the CI/CD process and in different deployment environments. Deployments are consistent and expected when artifacts are handled correctly.

#### 2.2. Greater speed of deployment

Artifacts that have already been built and tested can be quickly pushed to production and other environments. This cuts down on the time needed for setting up and configuring things by hand.

### 2.3. Going Back

Build artifacts let you go back to earlier versions of the software if there are problems withdeployment or mistakes that you didn't expect. This gives you a safety net during releases.

### 2.4. You can track it

Artifacts are linked to specific code commits and can be used to look back at the software's past. This makes it easier to find out when and where problems first appeared.

## III. The Best Ways to Handle Build Artifacts

### 3.1. Making versions

Each build file should have its own version. A popular way to show how important changes are

is through semantic versioning, which looks like this: MAJOR.MINOR.PATCH. Versioning correctly makes sure that artifacts can be tracked and lets you handle dependencies well.

### 3.2. Artifact Library

An artifact repository or artifact management system can be used to keep build files safe and organized. Some well-known options are JFrog Artifactory, Sonatype Nexus, and cloud-based services like Amazon S3, Google Cloud Storage, and Azure Blob Storage. Versioning, access control, and artifact metadata are some of the benefits that these repositories offer.

### 3.3. Data about artifacts

Include metadata with each product that lists what it contains, what it depends on, and how to build it. This metadata is useful for keeping track of artifacts and handling them well.

### 3.4. Publishing by Computer

Make it so that build artifacts are automatically added to the artifact repository as part of the CI process. In this way, artifacts are always and instantly made available for distribution and deployment.

### 3.5. Rules for keeping records

Set up retention rules to keep track of how long build artifacts are used. Set rules for how to clean up, archive, and delete artifacts based on things like version, age, and usage. Retention rules help keep artifact repositories organized and keep storage costs down.

## IV. Ways to Deal with Build Artifacts

### 4.1. Build Once, Use Many

Make sure that the artifacts created during the CI pipeline are used the same way in all environments, from development and testing to staging and production, by following the "build once, deploy many" rule. This cuts down on differences and makes distribution easier.

### 4.2. Ways to get promoted

Set up promotion routes that move build artifacts from testing to deployment and back again. To give you an idea, artifacts could be sent to a staging environment first, and then to production if testing goes well. Promotion pipelines help make sure that only artifacts that have been fully tested and approved make it to production.

### 4.3. Fixed Infrastructure

You might want to use immutable infrastructure, which means that the whole infrastructure, including the app and all of its dependencies, is viewed like code. This stops configuration drift and makes sure that every release uses the same set of build artifacts.

### 4.4. Management of Dependencies

Manage dependencies from one place to keep build files free of changes that were not expected. To list and handle dependencies, use tools for dependency management such as Maven, npm, or Pipenv.

### 4.5. Plan for rolling back

Have a clear plan for rolling back changes ready in case the launch fails or there are other problems. When you rollback, you should use the same build files to go back to the previous version of the app.

## V. Problems and Things to Think About

### 5.1. Size and Scalability of Artifacts

Large build artifacts can put a strain on bandwidth and storage, especially in CI/CD setups with multiple nodes. To deal with these problems, you might want to think about using artifact caching and binary stores.

### 5.2. Safety and Controlling Access

Make sure that only the right people can view the build artifacts. To keep private information safe, use access controls, authentication systems, and encryption.

### 5.3. Artifact Adequacy

Make sure that build results and the code they are linked to are always the same. Updates to the code should cause artifacts to be recreated so that they don't match.

### 5.4. Auditing and following rules

Depending on your business and the rules that apply to it, you may have to follow certain compliance standards when it comes to how you handle and store artifacts. Set up the right tracking and reporting systems to show that you are following the rules.

## VI. Tools and Services for Dealing with Build Artifacts

### 6.1. The JFrog Artifact

A well-known artifact storage manager, JFrog Artifactory works with many package types, such as Java, Docker, npm, and more. Versioning, access control, and managing information are all built into it.

6.2. The Sonatype Nexus

Sonatype Nexus is another popular artifact repository manager that works with a number of package types. It has tools for managing dependencies, hosting repositories, and controlling who can access them.

6.3. Amazon Web Services

AWS Simple Storage Service (S3) is an object storage service that can be used to store build data. It is scalable and highly available. It has tools for versioning and controlling who can see what.

6.4. Google Drive Store

Google Cloud Storage is an object storage service in the cloud that lets you store and manage build files safely and on an as-needed basis.

CI/CD processes need to be able to handle build artifacts well in order to stay consistent, reliable, and repeatable. Using best practices like versioning, artifact repositories, metadata, and retention policies, along with following best practices, development teams can make sure that build artifacts are handled well throughout the software development lifecycle. "Build once, deploy many" and promotion pipelines are two strategies that make software deployments even more reliable. When managed well and problems and rules for compliance are carefully thought through, build files can help you confidently deliver high-quality software.

5.4 CI/CD Security Best Practices

Continuous Integration and Continuous Deployment (CI/CD) have changed the way software is made and made it possible for companies to release software quickly and easily. But CI/CD systems' speed and ability to automate tasks make them hard to secure. We will talk about the best CI/CD security practices in this post to help you keep your software pipeline safe and secure.

1. Getting CI/CD right

1.1. What does CI/CD mean?

Continuous Integration (CI) and Continuous Deployment (CD) are ways of making software that stress automation and working together. Continuous integration (CI) builds, tests, and adds changes to code to a shared repository instantly. CD adds to CI by automating the process of putting code into production or other settings.

1.2. Important Parts of CI/CD

1. **Version Control:** A single place to store changes to code, like Git.
2. **Build Automation:** Compiling, testing, and packaging changes to code that are done automatically.
3. **Deployment Automation:** code changes are sent automatically to different locations.
4. **Automated Testing:** This includes unit testing, integration testing, and end-to-end testing.
5. **tracking and Feedback:** Issues are found and fixed through continuous tracking and feedback.

II. Why CI/CD security is important

2.1. Speed vs. Safety

CI/CD processes are made to work quickly and efficiently, but these very qualities can make them less safe. When automated processes add security holes by accident, and when code changes are made quickly, there may not be enough time for a security check.

2.2. Breach of security costs a lot

Security breaches can cost a company a lot of money and hurt its image. Security holes in CI/CD can let people in who aren't supposed to, leak data, or run harmful code.

2.3. Rules and compliance

Data security and compliance rules apply to a lot of different fields. A security hole in a CI/CD system can cause noncompliance, which can lead to fines and other legal issues.

III. Best Practices for CI/CD Security

3.1. Safety Tips for Coding

1. **Code Review:** Set up methods for reviewing code to find security holes before they are used in production.
2. **Static Analysis:** Fix bugs and security holes in your code instantly with static analysis tools.
3. **Security Libraries:** To stop common weaknesses like SQL injection, XSS, and CSRF attacks, use security libraries and frameworks that are well taken care of.
4. **Secure Coding Standards:** Make sure writers follow secure coding standards and train them on how to do so.

3.2. Controlling access based on roles

1. Use role-based access control (RBAC) to make sure that only people who are allowed to can access CI/CD pipelines and resources linked to them.
2. **Limit Privileges:** Use the principle of least privilege (PoLP) to make sure that people only have the access they need to do their jobs.
3. **Two-Factor Authentication:** Make sure that users who want to access CI/CD tools and files have to use two-factor authentication (2FA).

### 3.3. Keeping secrets safe

1. Encrypt critical data like API keys and passwords and keep it safe in vaults or key management systems.
2. **Don't Hardcode Secrets:** Never put secrets in code or setup files that you can't change. Put them in at runtime instead.
3. **Change Secrets:** To lower the risk of someone getting in without permission, change secrets and passwords on a regular basis.

### 3.4. Safety of Containers

1. **Scanning Images:** To find security holes in CI/CD container images, use tools that scan container images.
2. **Safe Registry:** Make sure that container images are kept in a safe registry for containers that only certain people can view.
3. **Least Privilege Containers:** To reduce the number of possible attack surfaces, set up containers using the concept of least privilege.

### 3.5. Monitoring All the Time

1. Make sure that CI/CD pipelines and environments are constantly monitored so that security issues can be found and dealt with in real time.
2. **Set Up Alerts:** Set up alerts for strange behavior, illegal access, or other problems.
3. **Log Analysis:** Look over logs on a regular basis to find possible security problems.

### 3.6. Safe Installation

1. **Immutable Infrastructure:** Use immutable infrastructure techniques to keep changes to the infrastructure safe and under control.

2. **Automated Deployment Verification:** To make sure that deployments meet security requirements, use automated methods for deployment verification and validation.
3. **Rollback Strategy:** Make a clear plan for how to go back to a known-good state in case there are security problems or breaches.

### 3.7. Security Testing All the Time

1. **Dynamic Application Security Testing (DAST):** To look for holes in running programs, use DAST tools.
2. **Runtime Application Self-Protection (RASP):** Use RASP tools to keep an eye on and protect apps while they're running.
3. **Penetration Testing:** Do penetration testing on a daily basis to find weak spots and holes.

### 3.8. Code-Based Safety

1. Use security as code (SAC) by writing down security rules and checks in CI/CD pipelines.
2. Use Infrastructure as Code (IaC) to describe and set up infrastructure that already has security controls built in.

### 3.9. Keep third-party dependencies safe

1. Keep third-party sources up to date so that known security holes are fixed.
2. Use dependency scanning tools to find weak spots in third-party libraries and packages and fix them.

## IV. Security Tools and Tech for CI/CD
### 4.1. OWASP Check for Dependencies
The OWASP Dependency-Check tool checks the dependencies on a project for known security holes.
### 4.2. The OWASP ZAP
A well-known open-source security testing tool for finding holes in web apps is OWASP ZAP (Zed Attack Proxy).
### 4.3. The Anchore Engine
Anchore Engine looks at container images and finds security holes.
### 4.4. The SonarQube
SonarQube is a tool for checking the quality and security of code all the time.

### 4.5. The GitLab CI/CD tool

GitLab CI/CD has security checking built in for both code and container images.

## V. Problems and Things to Think About

### 5.1. Finding the Right Speed and Safety Balance

In CI/CD environments, it's always hard to find the right mix between fast development and strong security. Security must be a top priority for organizations without slowing down the rollout process.

### 5.2. Requirements for Compliance

Compliance rules are different for each industry and area. CI/CD pipelines need to be able to change to meet these unique rules.

### 5.3. Changes in Culture

CI/CD security works best when both the development and operations teams are responsible for security and know how to keep it safe.

CI/CD security is very important in today's fast-paced software development world. Security breaches can cause a lot of problems, like losing money and hurting your image. Companies can protect their software processes and give their users safe and reliable software by following CI/CD security best practices, using the right tools, and creating a culture that values security.

# Chapter 6

## Continuous Deployment in the Cloud

Continuous Deployment, or CD, is a way of making software that has completely changed how apps are released and updated. Continuous Deployment in the Cloud, along with the power of cloud computing, has changed the game for businesses that want to speed up software release, improve product quality, and stay competitive in today's fast-paced digital world.

This article will go into detail about the idea of Continuous Deployment in the Cloud, looking at its principles, pros and cons, best practices, and examples from real life. By the end, you'll know everything you need to know about how CD in the Cloud can change the way you build and release software.

How to Understand Continuous Deployment

Continuous Deployment is a way of making software that focuses on automating the process of putting new changes to code into production as soon as they are ready. This method makes sure that users get software changes quickly and easily, with little to no manual work needed.

Important rules for continuous deployment:

1. **Automation:** Continuous Deployment is based on automation. It uses automated tests, build, and deployment pipelines to make sure that changes to the code can be put into production without any help from a person. Automation speeds up the shipping process and lowers the chance of mistakes made by people.
2. **Continuous Integration (CI):** CI is the process of adding changes to code to a public repository on a regular basis. Every time new code is added, automated tests are run to find problems quickly. CI

# CLOUD-BASED CI/CD FOR SOFTWARE TEAMS — 121

is needed for Continuous Deployment because it makes sure that changes to the code are always ready to be deployed.

3. **Automated Testing:** It is important to use automated testing to make sure that changes to the code don't cause problems or regressions. Unit tests, integration tests, and end-to-end tests are all part of test suites that are run regularly as part of the deployment pipeline.
4. **Change Tracking:** Systems like Git are used to keep track of changes made to the software. They keep track of all changes to the code and make it easier for teams to work together.

Continuous Deployment in the Cloud Pros:

1. **Faster Time to Market:** With CD in the Cloud, companies can quickly give people new features and updates. This flexibility is very important in today's market, where being able to quickly meet customer wants can make a big difference.
2. **Better quality:** Continuous integration and automated testing make sure that all changes to the code are tested fully before they are released. This improves the quality of the program and cuts down on production problems.
3. **Less risk:** Because CD automates the process, it lowers the risk that comes with manual deploys. It's also easy to do rollbacks if something goes wrong, which lowers risk even more.
4. **Continuous Feedback:** When companies release their products more often, they can get feedback from users more quickly. This helps them make better decisions and improve their products.

Problems that come up with continuous deployment in the cloud:

1. **Complexity of the infrastructure:** It can be hard to manage cloud infrastructure when there are a lot of services and settings to deal with. Infrastructure as Code (IaC) can help make this problem less of a problem.
2. **Cultural Shift:** For CD to work, companies need to change the way they do things. In traditional development settings, it can be hard for teams to accept automation and continuous improvement.
3. **Worries about security:** Quick operations can make people worry about security. It's important to build security into the CD pipeline and check cloud resources for holes on a daily basis.

4. **Problems with Compatibility:** CD may find problems with how well it works with different cloud services or deployment settings. To fix these kinds of problems, thorough testing is a must.

The best ways to do continuous deployment in the cloud are:

1. **Make a strong CI/CD pipeline:** Spend money on a clear CI/CD pipeline that includes testing, deployment, and tracking that are all done automatically. This pipeline should be able to grow as needed and change to new needs.
2. **Adopt Infrastructure as Code (IaC):** To handle cloud resources, use IaC tools such as Terraform or AWS CloudFormation. This makes sure that your system is consistent and can be used again and again.
3. **Set up automatic testing:** Make a full set of automated tests to make sure that changes to the code are correct at every step of the deployment process.
4. **Monitor and Analyze:** Use monitoring and logging to learn more about how well a service is running. Use this information to find problems early and make the application work better.

Examples of Continuous Deployment in the Cloud in the Real World:

1. **Netflix:** Netflix was one of the first companies to use cloud-native apps, and it uses Continuous Deployment to send material and updates to its users all over the world. To keep a high level of availability and user experience, they use microservices design and a lot of automated testing.
2. **Amazon Web Services (AWS):** One company that uses CD to release changes to its cloud services is AWS itself. This shows that CD can be used to handle the infrastructure that makes other cloud services work.
3. **Etsy:** The e-commerce company Etsy uses CD to make changes to its website. They encourage people to try new things all the time and use feature flags to slowly give new features to users.

Continuous Deployment in the Cloud is a new way to deliver software that uses automation, cloud computing, and current ways of building software. It lets companies put out software quickly while keeping the quality good and responding well to user feedback. There are some problems with CD in the Cloud, but there are also many benefits that make it an important strategy for keeping competitive in today's fast-paced digital world.

## 6.1 Configuring CD Environments

Continuous Delivery (CD) is an important part of current software development because it helps teams make high-quality software quickly and easily. Setting up environments is a key part of making CD work. They are what make the deployment process automatic, make sure consistency, and lower the risk of mistakes. This piece will talk about why setting up CD environments is important and what the best ways are to do it.

### What CD environments do

As the name suggests, this is where programmers write and check their code. It works the same way as local development and is very important for finding problems early on in the development process.

**Integration Environment:** This is where changes to the code made by different developers or teams are tried and put into the main code. This setting helps find problems and clashes with integration.

**Testing/Staging Environment:** This is a copy of the production environment where full testing takes place, such as speed, security, and functionality testing. It makes sure the code is ready to be used in production.

**Production Environment:** This is where real people use your app or service. Changes are only made here after they have been tested thoroughly in other places.

### Advantages of Setting Up Your CD Environment Correctly

**Consistency:** Setups are the same across all environments, so differences between development, test, and production settings are less likely to cause problems.

**Automation:** Configuration as code (IaC), also known as "Infrastructure as Code," lets environments be set up and managed automatically, so mistakes that happen during human setup are avoided.

**Traceability:** The right setup lets you keep track of changes made to the environment settings, which helps with testing and troubleshooting.

**Repeatability:** It's easy to make new environments, which makes testing and fixing problems easier.

**Security:** All environments can be made to use secure configurations, which lowers risks and makes sure compliance.

### Best Practices for Setting Up CD Environments

1. Use IaC (Infrastructure as Code)

   Tools for infrastructure configuration management (IaC) like Terraform, Ansible, and AWS CloudFormation make it easy to set up and control how infrastructure works. When you use IaC, settings are thought of as code, which means they can be repeated, tracked by version, and run automatically. Changes to surroundings are easier to see, which makes them easier to track.

2. **Don't mix configuration and code.**
Keep application code and management code separate. This keeps your CD pipeline clean and makes it easy to change settings for the environment without changing the code. To do this, you can use setup files, environment variables, or third-party configuration tools.

3. **Explain what configuration templates are**
Make models for different kinds of settings. There could be a design for a web server, a database server, or a load balancer, among other things. You should add parameters to these templates so that you can use them again with different settings.

4. **Keep track of your configurations' versions**
You should keep track of different versions of your code and the settings for your surroundings in the same way. This makes sure that you can keep track of changes, go back to earlier versions of things, and work together with your team successfully.

5. **Set up environments automatically**
Use automation tools to set up and take care of your settings. One way to manage the deployment process is to use Jenkins, Travis CI, or CircleCI. Human error is cut down and uniformity is maintained through automation.

6. **Follow the best practices for security**
In CD settings, security is very important. Use the least privilege principle, encrypt private data, and check for vulnerabilities on a regular basis as security best practices. Using security as code (SaC) helps make sure that all environments have a safe configuration.

7. **Keep an eye on and check the configurations**
It is important to keep an eye on how the setting is configured all the time. Set up auditing tools to find changes that were not made by approved users and to make sure that security policies and best practices are being followed.

8. **Setups for tests**
You should test your setup like you would code. Make sure that any changes you make to the configuration templates don't cause problems in your CD workflow. Before releasing configurations, use automated testing tools to make sure they work.

9. **Use orchestration and containers**
Containers, like Docker, and tools for managing containers, like Kubernetes, make it possible to launch and scale applications

consistently in a variety of settings. They make it easier to handle configurations and make things more portable.
10. Setting up documents

For sharing information, fixing problems, and getting new team members up to speed, it's important to keep detailed records of how the environment is set up. To keep documents up to date, use tools like wikis or markdown files.

How to Avoid Common Mistakes

**Manual setup:** If you rely on manual setup, mistakes and inconsistencies will happen. The key is automation.

**Ignoring Security:** If you don't pay attention to security in settings, your application could be vulnerable.

**Not Version Controlling settings:** If you don't version control settings, it's hard to keep track of changes and work together efficiently.

**Not Enough Testing:** Not doing enough configuration testing can lead to problems and mistakes that aren't seen until deployment.

**Lack of guidance:** Configurations are hard to understand and fix when there isn't enough guidance.

For software transfer to work, CD environments must be set up correctly. You can make sure that your deployment process is consistent, secure, and easy to track by using Infrastructure as Code, keeping configuration separate from code, and following best practices. Keep in mind that one of the main ideas behind CD is continuous improvement. To keep up with changing technologies and needs, you should review and update your environment configurations on a regular basis. You can safely and quickly give your users high-quality software if your CD environments are set up correctly.

6.2 Deploying Applications Automatically

In the constantly changing world of software development, instantly deploying apps has become a game-changer. There are many benefits to automating the release process, such as making it faster, more reliable, and more consistent. This piece goes into detail about automatic application deployment, including what it means, how to do it right, and the tools that make it possible.

Why automatic application deployment is important

1. Speed and ease of use
   The time it takes to go from committing code to production is cut down by automating the launch process. In the fast-paced world of

development we live in now, getting new features and bug fixes to users quickly can give you an edge over your competitors.

2. **Sticking to it**
   Manual deployments can make settings not work the same way, which can lead to "it works on my machine" situations. With automatic deployment, the same steps are always taken, so the development, testing, and production settings are all the same.
3. **Less mistakes**
   When transfers are done by hand, mistakes are common. By automating the process, these mistakes are taken care of, which leads to more reliable releases and a lower chance of costly outages or security holes.
4. **The ability to roll back**
   A lot of automatic deployment tools have ways to undo changes. If a problem appears after deployment, it is easy to go back to a previous version, which limits the amount of downtime and user impact.
5. **CI/CD stands for Continuous Integration and Delivery.**

An important part of CI/CD systems is automatic deployment. CI/CD encourages a culture of continuous integration and testing, making sure that changes to the code are instantly built, tested, and deployed as soon as they are ready.

**The best ways to set up automatic application deployment**

1. **Set up a CI/CD pipeline**
   A CI/CD workflow makes it easy to build, test, and release your app all at once. When new code is committed, tools like Jenkins, Travis CI, GitLab CI/CD, and GitHub Actions can be used to build strong workflows that run deployments automatically.
2. **Infrastructure as Code**
   To describe and set up the infrastructure your app needs, use Infrastructure as Code (IaC) tools like Terraform or AWS CloudFormation. This makes sure that your infrastructure is the same in all settings and can be used again and again.
3. **Keep track of changes**
   Keep track of different versions of your application code, configuration files, and release scripts. This lets you keep track of changes, work together well, and go back to earlier versions if something goes wrong.
4. **Isolating the environment**
   Keep the environments for development, testing, and release

separate. Isolation keeps problems in one setting from spreading to others and gives you a safe place to test updates.
5. Testing that is done automatically
Automated testing should be part of your deployment process. This includes unit tests, integration tests, and end-to-end tests to find problems quickly and make sure your app works as it should in all settings.
6. Implementations of Blue-Green
You can use blue-green deployments, which have two similar environments. One will run the current version (blue), and the other will run the new version (green). By switching between them, you can cut down on downtime and quickly go back if you need to.
7. Canary Lets Go
You might want to use "canary releases," which involve slowly giving new features or updates to a small group of people. This lets you see how changes affect things and get comments before a full deployment.
8. Watching and keeping records
Set up strong methods for monitoring and logging. You can find problems in real time, fix them, and learn a lot about how well your application is running with tools like Prometheus, Grafana, and ELK stack.
9. Safety with Code
"Security as Code" (SaC) says that you should build security checks into your deployment process. To make sure your app is safe, you should include automated security scans and vulnerability assessments in the way you release it.
10. Proof of ownership

Write down everything about your deployment method, such as the steps, settings, and dependencies. It's easier for team members to understand and keep up with the deployment pipeline when processes are well recorded.

Tools for deploying apps automatically

1. Google Cloud
Kubernetes is a powerful platform for orchestrating containers that makes it easy to launch, scale, and manage containerized apps. In different environments, it gives you a consistent way to set up and handle apps.

2. No Docker
   Docker makes it easier to put apps and the libraries they need into containers. Then, it's easy to install and run these containers in different environments, making sure that they are consistent and portable.
3. Jarvis
   Jenkins is a well-known open-source automation service that makes it easier to write, test, and release code. A lot of different tools and plugins work well with it, which makes it a good choice for CI/CD processes.
4. CI/CD and GitLab
   Because GitLab CI/CD is built in, it has a continuous integration and delivery platform that makes it easier to automate deployment processes. It works very well with GitLab's features for managing versions and keeping track of issues.
5. This is AWS Elastic Beanstalk
   AWS Elastic Beanstalk makes it easier to set up and run AWS applications. It hides the specifics of the infrastructure so that writers can focus on writing code. Scaling and load balancing are handled automatically.
6. DevOps in Azure
   Azure DevOps is a complete set of tools for automating the launch of apps on the Microsoft Azure cloud platform. Version control, CI/CD, and program monitoring are all built into it.
7. The CircleI
   CircleCI is a CI/CD platform that runs in the cloud and automates the deployment process. A lot of computer languages can be used with it, and it works with well-known version control systems.
8. The spinnaker

Spinnaker is a continuous delivery tool made by Netflix that is open source and works across multiple clouds. It can be automatically deployed to different cloud providers, which makes it perfect for businesses with complicated infrastructures that use more than one cloud.

An important part of modern software creation is automatic application deployment. It speeds up the release process, makes it more efficient, and lowers the chance of mistakes. By following best practices and using the right tools, companies can not only get software to users faster, but they can also make it more secure and reliable. As technology keeps getting better, automating release will remain an important way to stay competitive in the fast-paced world of software development.

## 6.3 Managing Rollbacks and Roll-forwards

Managing rollbacks and roll-forwards is an important skill to have in the complicated world of software creation and deployment. These steps help companies deal with problems and changes to their software versions that they didn't expect. This piece talks about rollbacks and roll-forwards, what they mean, the best ways to use them, and the tools that can assist businesses with these important areas of software administration.

### How to Understand Roll-backs and Roll-forwards

#### Going back

A rollback is the process of going back to an earlier version or state of a software tool or system. When major problems like software bugs, security holes, or speed issues are found after a new version or update has been released, this is usually what is done. Rollbacks are meant to get the system back to a stable and working state by "undoing" the changes that were made in the most recent release.

#### Forward rolls

When you roll-forward, on the other hand, you move a system to a newer version or state. This can be done to install bug changes, security patches, or improvements that are needed to keep the system running well or make it work better. Roll-forwards aim to move to a state that is thought to be more stable and helpful, while rollbacks try to go back to a known-good state.

### Why rollbacks and rollforwards are important

#### Why rollbacks are important:

**Risk Reduction:** Rollbacks are a safety net that helps companies lower the risks that come with releasing new software. A rollback can quickly fix a system that isn't stable after a launch goes wrong.

**Lessening Downtime:** Rollbacks can cut down on downtime caused by unplanned problems, so users can still access the app or service.

**Security:** If there are security holes or breaches, rollbacks can quickly go back to an older, safer version, keeping user data and information safe.

**Maintaining Customer Trust:** Fixing problems quickly and getting back to a working state helps keep customers' trust by reducing downtime and making sure users have a good experience.

#### Why roll-forwards are important:

**Bug Fixes and Improvements:** Roll-forwards let companies quickly apply important bug fixes, security changes, and feature improvements, which makes the system more stable and useful overall.

**Compliance:** In businesses that are regulated, keeping up with changing rules may require regular roll-forwards to make sure systems are secure and up to date.

**Advantage in the Market:** Businesses can get an edge over their competitors by quickly adding new features and changes to their software through roll-forwards.

**Scalability:** Roll-forwards can be used to make apps bigger to handle more users or more work, making sure the system can handle more demand.

How to handle rollbacks and roll-forwards in the best way possible

1. **Computerization**
   Automate the steps of both rolling back and forward. These tasks can be done quickly and accurately by automated scripts or orchestration tools, which lowers the chance of mistakes made by people.
2. **Keep track of changes**
   Keep your code and settings safe by using a strong version control system. During rollbacks, this makes it easy to find and go back to earlier states when needed.
3. **CI/CD stands for Continuous Integration and Continuous Deployment.**
   CI/CD processes can be used to test and release new versions automatically. As a result, new changes are fully tested before they are put into production, which makes rollbacks less likely.
4. **Places for staging**
   For testing, use staging environments that are very similar to your production system. This lets you find problems before they get to the production setting, which means you don't have to do as many rollbacks.
5. **Watching over and warning**
   Set up complete monitoring and alerting systems to find and fix problems in production fast. When needed, automated alerts can cause rollbacks or forwards.
6. **Saving and getting back**
   Back up important info and settings on a regular basis. This makes sure that you always have a good place to start with rollbacks and that you can quickly get back on track after something goes wrong.
7. **Plan to go back**
   Make a well-thought-out rollback plan that spells out the steps to take if something goes wrong during rollout. Make sure that everyone on your team knows the plan and can carry it out well.
8. **Talking to people**
   Keep the lines of communication open and clear with all parties, such as end users, development teams, and operations teams. Tell

them about any planned rollbacks or forwards and keep them up to date on the deployment's progress.
9. Validation and testing

Both rollback and rollforward processes should be tested thoroughly in non-production environments to make sure they work. This helps find and fix any problems that might come up before they affect production.

Tools for keeping track of rollbacks and forwards

1. Systems for keeping track of changes
   Version control systems (VCS) like Git and Subversion let you keep different versions of code and setup files. This makes it easier to keep track of changes and undo them when you need to.
2. Platforms for CI/CD
   The deployment process is automated by CI/CD systems like Jenkins, Travis CI, GitLab CI/CD, and CircleCI. This makes it easier to plan rollbacks and roll-forwards.
3. Containerization and putting things together
   Containers (like Docker) and container orchestration platforms (like Kubernetes) make roll-forwards easier by making it simple to handle and grow application parts.
4. Tools for backup and recovery
   Backup programs like Veeam, Acronis, and AWS Backup can protect and restore data and allow you to go back to earlier states.
5. Tools for monitoring and alerting
   Monitoring tools like Prometheus, Grafana, and Nagios show you how healthy your system is in real time and can roll back changes based on rules you set.
6. Tools for managing configurations

Tools like Ansible, Puppet, and Chef make it easier to handle configurations across environments and make sure they are all the same.

Managing rollbacks and roll-forwards is important for keeping the system stable, making sure it's secure, and giving users a good experience in the ever-changing world of software release. Companies can confidently handle the complicated world of software management by sticking to best practices, automating tasks where possible, and using the right tools. Rollbacks are a safety net for fixing problems that come up out of the blue, and roll-forwards make it easy to quickly apply important changes and improvements. Together, these strategies give businesses the tools they need to adapt and do well in a software environment that is always changing.

### 6.4 Monitoring Deployed Applications

Monitoring apps that have been deployed is an important part of modern software development and operations. It means keeping an eye on the performance, availability, and security of a service all the time. Monitoring that works well not only helps find problems before they happen, but it also lets you make decisions based on data, improve performance, and make users happier. This piece will talk about why monitoring deployed applications is important, as well as best practices, key metrics, and the tools and technologies that make monitoring work well.

**Why monitoring deployed applications is important**

1. **Finding problems early on**
   With proactive tracking, you can find problems and fix them before they affect end users. This means finding problems with performance, system outages, security holes, and program errors.
2. **Better experience for users**
   Monitoring makes sure that your app is always accessible, quick to respond, and dependable. This makes the user experience good, which is important for keeping customers happy and coming back.
3. **Improving things**
   Continuous monitoring gives you useful information that you can use to make your application and infrastructure more efficient, find speed bottlenecks, and make the best use of your resources.
4. **Safety**
   Monitoring helps find security holes and strange behavior early on, so that actions can be taken quickly to limit the damage that could happen.
5. **Making decisions based on data**

Monitoring can collect data that can be used to help make decisions. This can help teams organize development work, make good use of resources, and make smart choices about how to improve infrastructure and applications.

**The best ways to keep an eye on deployed apps**

1. **Make your goals clear**
   First, write down your goals for tracking. What parts of your app do you need to keep an eye on the most? Know what your key performance indicators (KPIs) mean and how to achieve them.

2. Pick Metrics That Are Useful
   Pick measures that help you reach your goals. Response time, error rates, resource usage (CPU, memory, disk, network), and user activity are all common metrics. Change your metrics so they fit the specifics of your program.
3. Keep an eye on the whole stack
   Keep an eye on the whole technology stack, from the application code to the computers, databases, and networks that hold the data. This all-around view helps you find problems more correctly.
4. Set alerts and thresholds
   Set levels for your data and set up systems that will send you alerts when they go over these levels. Alerts should be actionable and describe the problem and possible answers.
5. Watch in real time
   With real-time tracking, you can fix problems quickly. Use tools that give you real-time information about how your application is doing and how healthy it is.
6. Put in place automated cleanup
   You might want to use automated answers to common problems. Like starting up a failed service instantly or changing the amount of resources based on demand.
7. Spread Out Tracing
   Track and look at requests as they move through your service with distributed tracing tools. This helps find problems with delay and bottlenecks.
8. Putting together logs
   Logs from your program and infrastructure should all be collected in one place. This makes troubleshooting and testing go more smoothly.
9. Analysis of past data and trends
   To find trends over time, collect and store tracking data from the past. Trend analysis can show long-term problems with performance or the need to plan for more capacity.
10. Review and update often

Review your monitoring plan every so often to make sure it still fits with your new goals and technologies. As needed, make changes to your tracking tools and settings.

Key Metrics for Keeping an Eye on Deployed Apps

1. **Time to Respond**
   Response time is a way to see how fast your app answers user requests. It's an important measure of how happy users are.
2. **Rate of Error**
   The error rate shows what fraction of requests fail or give errors. Keeping an eye on this measure helps you find problems in your application and fix them.
3. **Making use of resources**
   Metrics for resource utilization, such as CPU, memory, disk, and network usage, show how well your system and applications are using resources.
4. **Being available and being online**
   Keeping an eye on your app's availability and uptime helps make sure that users can still access it. Keep track of breakdowns and downtime to fix problems with reliability.
5. **Pace of flow**
   Throughput is a way to figure out how many calls your app can handle in a certain amount of time. It's important for planning and optimizing capacity.
6. **Time Delay**
   Metrics for latency show how long it takes for a request to move through your app. When delay is high, it can affect how users feel.
7. **What the user does**
   Knowing about user activity, like the number of current users, the demographics of those users, and how they use the site, can help you make features and performance better.
8. **Logs of errors**

Keeping an eye on error logs can help you find and fix program errors and exceptions. It's important for fixing bugs and making the code better.

**Technologies and tools for keeping an eye on deployed apps**

1. **Grafana and Prometheus**
   Grafana lets you see what's happening and make dashboards, and Prometheus is an open-source tracking and alerting toolkit. Together, they make a strong way to keep an eye on numbers and see what they mean.
2. **Elastic Stack**
   A lot of people use the ELK Stack, which is made up of Elasticsearch, Logstash, and Kibana, to collect and analyze logs. This makes it easier to organize and find logs.

3. Brand New
   New Relic offers complete tools for application performance monitoring (APM). It gives you real-time information about how applications work and how they behave.
4. The Datadog
   Datadog has a single monitoring platform that handles APM, infrastructure monitoring, and log handling. It lets you see how services and infrastructure are running in real time.
5. The Splunk
   Splunk is a flexible platform that can be used to find, monitor, and analyze data from security systems, applications, and infrastructure. It's useful for keeping an eye on both operations and security.
6. Dynamic Apps
   APM solutions from AppDynamics let you keep an eye on how well apps are running and how users are feeling about them. It gives you information about how applications work and how to track transactions.
7. Nagios
   Nagios is a well-known open-source monitoring system that lets you keep an eye on network devices, servers, and services. It has the ability to inform and notify users.
8. CloudWatch from AWS
   AWS CloudWatch is an official AWS tool for keeping an eye on AWS apps and resources. It gives metrics, logs, and alarms for custom apps hosted on AWS and AWS services.
9. You can watch Google Cloud
   The Google Cloud Monitoring service keeps an eye on and records what's going on with Google Cloud. Monitoring, logging, and tracking Google Cloud services and apps are all possible with it.
10. Azure Watch

Azure Monitor is the service that keeps an eye on and fixes problems with Microsoft Azure. It gives you information about how well apps and infrastructure hosted on Azure are running and whether they are healthy.

Monitoring installed applications is an important part of making sure they work well, are reliable, and are safe. Monitoring that works well lets companies find problems before they happen, make the best use of their resources, and improve the user experience. By using tracking tools and technologies and following best practices, you can learn a lot about how your application works, make decisions based on data, and make sure that your software deployments continue to go well. Monitoring isn't just a good idea in today's fast-paced and always-changing tech world; it's a must if you want to stay competitive and meet user standards.

# Chapter 7

## Advanced CI/CD Topics

CI/CD, which stands for Continuous Integration and Continuous Deployment, has changed the way software is built and distributed. These techniques are now standard in modern software development and help teams make, test, and release software more quickly and better. We will go beyond the basics and look at the details and best practices that can help you take your CI/CD process to the next level in this in-depth look at Advanced CI/CD topics.

### The Beginning

Continuous Deployment (CD) and Continuous Integration (CI) have come a long way since they
were first used. Even though the basic ideas behind CI/CD (automate, integrate, and deploy often) haven't changed, new topics and methods have come up to deal with the complexity of modern software development. We will talk about these more advanced CI/CD topics in this detailed guide. We will give you tips, methods, and the best ways to run your CI/CD pipelines.

### It stands for Infrastructure as Code.

### Figuring out IaC

A key part of complex CI/CD is infrastructure as code (IaC). It includes using code and automation scripts to manage and set up infrastructure. If you understand IaC, you can describe your infrastructure in a way that is version-controlled and can be used again and again.

### Adding support for CI/CD

Find out how to add IaC to your CI/CD workflow. You can make sure that your environments are uniform across development, testing, and production by thinking of infrastructure as code. This lowers the chance of deployment problems.

### Good and Bad Things About It

Check out the advantages of IaC, such as more adaptability, scalability, and less need for physical work. But also be aware of the problems, like the fact that it takes time to learn and that you need to test things properly.

### Making music and automating tasks

### Advanced Orchestration of Workflow

For advanced CI/CD processes to work, the workflow needs to be carefully coordinated. Find out how to manage dependencies, handle parallelism, and organize complex deployment methods.

### Making deployment tasks automatic

CI/CD is based on automating things. You can make sure that deployments are consistent and error-free by learning how to automate chores like database migrations and configuration management.

### Tools and building blocks

Check out well-known CI/CD automation and orchestration tools and systems like GitLab CI/CD, CircleCI, and Jenkins to learn what makes them good and bad.

### Setting up containers and CI/CD

### Docker and Making Containers

Containerization has changed how applications are packaged and deployed in a big way. Learn about Docker and the idea of containerization. Also, learn how containers work in CI/CD processes.

### Containers being added to CI/CD

Read about the best ways to add containers to your CI/CD process. You can learn about image versioning, container registries, and how to use container orchestration tools.

### Orchestration for Kubernetes and Containers

As of now, Kubernetes is the usual way to orchestrate containers. Check out how Kubernetes can improve your CI/CD processes by making them more resilient and scalable.

### With CI/CD and microservices

### Architecture for Microservices

Microservices are becoming more popular because they can be changed quickly and can grow as needed. Learn how microservices design works and how it affects CI/CD.

### Problems with CI/CD in Microservices

Learn about the difficulties of using CI/CD in a microservices setting, such as finding services, managing versions, and coordinating them.

### Tips for Getting CI/CD to Work in Microservices

Find out how to set up successful CI/CD pipelines in a microservices environment, such as how to do canary deployments and blue-green deployments.

### Safety in CI/CD

#### The rules of DevSecOps

When making new software, security is very important. Find out about the ideas behind DevSecOps and how you can use them in your CI/CD processes.

#### Testing for security in CI/CD

Find out about the different types of security testing, such as static analysis, dynamic analysis, and penetration testing, and how to make your process more automated.

#### Protected Management of Secrets

It is very important for security to keep track of secrets like API keys and passwords. Look into the best ways to handle secrets in CI/CD, such as using tools like AWS Secrets Manager and HashiCorp Vault.

### Testing for performance in CI/CD

#### Why performance testing is important

Performance is a very important part of program quality. Learn why speed testing is important and how it affects the user experience and the dependability of the system.

#### Performance testing being added to CI/CD

Find out how to automate load testing, add performance testing to your CI/CD workflow, and look at the results.

#### Tools and ways of working

Check out well-known performance testing tools and methods, like JMeter, Gatling, and APM (Application Performance Monitoring) options.

### Monitoring and being able to see

#### Monitoring in real time

With real-time monitoring, you can see how your program is working. Learn how to set up tracking systems that work in real time so that problems can be found and fixed quickly.

#### Collection and Analysis of Logs

Log handling is a very important part of troubleshooting and debugging. Look into tools and methods for collecting and analyzing logs.

#### Continuous Improvement by Being Able to See

Observability is a way of looking at system activity as a whole. Find out how observability can help your CI/CD processes get better all the time.

### Deployments in Multiple Environments

#### Taking care of several environments

It takes careful management to deal with various environments, like development, staging, and production. Figure out how to stay consistent in different settings.

### Advanced Strategies for Deployment

Learn about more advanced release methods, such as feature toggles, canary deployments, and blue-green deployments, and when to use each one.

### Setting up Canary and Blue-Green

Learn about the ideas behind canary and blue-green deployments and how they can help you minimize downtime and risk during deployments.

### How to Make CI/CD Work for Big Projects

### Big projects can be hard for CI/CD

Complexity and scaling problems often come up with big projects. Find out how to deal with these problems and make your CI/CD processes work well at a larger scale.

### Strategies for Scalability

Look into ways to make CI/CD processes bigger, such as using distributed builds, caching, and parallelization.

### CI/CD systems that are spread out

Find out about distributed CI/CD tools that can handle big projects and teams that work in different places.

### Being compliant and auditing

### Making sure CI/CD is compliant

It is important to follow the rules and policies set by the company. Learn how to make sure that your CI/CD processes are compliant by doing things like controlling who can see what and reviewing them.

### Tracks and reports for audits

For regulatory reasons, you need to learn how to keep audit trails and make compliance reports.

### Regulatory Things to Think About

Look into regulatory issues in CI/CD, like GDPR, HIPAA, and compliance needs that are specific to your business.

### Pipelines for CI/CD as Code

### Building Blocks as Code for CI/CD

Include the idea of "Infrastructure as Code" in your CI/CD processes. Find out why defining your CI/CD processes as code is a good idea.

### Pros and Best Practices

Find out about the benefits of thinking of CI/CD processes as code, such as controlling versions, reviewing code, and being able to make changes again and again.

### Useful Tips and Examples

Check out examples of CI/CD pipelines written in code, as well as the systems and tools that support this method, like GitLab CI/CD configuration as code and Jenkinsfile.

More advanced CI/CD in the cloud

Using services in the cloud

There are many services that can make your CI/CD processes better that are available in the cloud. Learn how to use cloud services to make your business more flexible and streamlined.

CI/CD without servers

Learn about the idea of serverless CI/CD, in which CI/CD tasks are run as needed using serverless computing.

Taking care of cloud resources with code

Learn about tools like AWS CloudFormation and Terraform that let you manage cloud resources as code, making sure that everything is the same every time.

7.1 Blue/Green Deployments

Agility and dependability are very important in the world of software creation and deployment. In order to keep up with users' ever-growing needs, businesses need to find ways to add new features and changes without causing problems. Blue/green deployments have become a powerful way to find this careful balance. They let teams make changes without any problems while reducing risks and downtime.

How Blue/Green Deployments Work

In the world of DevOps and continuous delivery, blue/green launches are a way to set up apps. The idea is pretty simple: you take care of two different worlds, one called "Blue" and the other "Green." The current production version of your app is in the blue environment. The green environment is where you add the new features, changes, or updates. What's great about this method is that it can help with the change from one environment to another without stopping end users' service.

The Blue Stage

In the beginning of a Blue/Green deployment, users interact with the live form of your app in the Blue environment. It's the production environment, which has been tested and is stable, so customers can access the app without any problems. The Green world, on the other hand, stays still, ready for the changes that are coming.

The Stage of Green

The Green environment is updated with the most recent code and settings as soon as the testing and development of new features or changes is done. This setting now has the version of the app that you want to make public. It's important to note that this environment goes through a lot of testing before it can be used by anyone. This testing includes functional, speed, and security testing. This makes sure that any bugs or problems are found and fixed before they affect the end users.

### The Change

A smooth change from the Blue environment to the Green environment is important for a Blue/Green rollout to work. Usually, this switch is made by changing the routing or load balancing settings so that data goes from the Blue environment to the Green environment. This step can be started by hand or automatically, based on the needs of the organization and their confidence in the deployment.

### Watching and Going Back

After the move, monitoring is very important. The Green setting is constantly being checked to make sure it's working as planned and that no problems have come up that weren't expected after it was set up. If any issues are found, the rollback process can be started by simply moving the routing or load balancing settings back to the Blue environment. This will take the program back to its previous version. This easy-to-use rollback feature lowers the risk of deployments and gives businesses a safety net.

### Pros and Cons of Blue/Green Deployments

### None of the time

One of the best things about Blue/Green operations is that they don't require any downtime. Users don't notice any changes to their service because the Green environment is fully tried and ready before it is switched on. This is especially important for applications that need to be open 24 hours a day, seven days a week, like e-commerce platforms, online services, and important business applications.

### Getting rid of risks

When you use blue/green launches, the risk that comes with new releases is greatly reduced. Possible problems can be found and fixed without hurting users by thoroughly testing the Green environment before sending traffic to it. If there is a problem, the switch can be quickly returned to the stable Blue setting, which will have the least amount of effect on the users.

### Better testing

Blue/Green deployments separate settings, which makes it easier to test thoroughly. As a specific testing ground for new changes, the Green environment lets for more thorough testing scenarios and makes sure that the deployment is of high quality before it reaches the users.

### Ability to Roll Back

As a safety net, being able to easily go back to the previous version of the app is very helpful. The development and management teams are confident because of this feature; they know they can quickly fix any problems that come up.

### More rapid releases

A faster release cycle is helped by blue/green pushes. You don't have to spend time setting up the production environment during the release window because the Green environment is always ready to go. In businesses that move quickly, this flexibility can give you an edge.

### How to Scale

When you use Blue/Green deployments, it's easier to make your app bigger. You can set up the Green environment to scale horizontally or vertically as needed to make sure the system can handle growth. This is useful if the new version of the app is expected to handle more users.

### The best ways to do blue and green deployments

### Make everything automatic

For a Blue/Green deployment method to work, it needs to be automated. Set up environments, publish code, and switch between Blue and Green environments automatically. Automation keeps things consistent, cuts down on mistakes made by people, and speeds up the release process.

### Tests for Everything

Testing is an important part of both Blue and Green operations. Make sure that your testing includes more than just basic testing. It should also include performance, security, and compatibility testing. This process can be made easier with the help of automated testing systems.

### Rollouts in Steps

In a green setting, you might want to think about using gradual rollouts. Instead of releasing all the changes at once, give some users new benefits over time. This lets testing happen in the real world and can help find problems that wouldn't show up in a normal testing setting.

### Monitoring and being able to see

Set up strong tracking and observability tools to keep an eye on both the Blue and Green environments' health and performance. Real-time data and reports can help find problems early and give you ideas for how to make things better.

### Write down the steps

Write down everything you need to know about your Blue/Green deployment method. This guide should go over every step, from setting up the environment to how to roll back changes. Having clear paperwork makes sure that everyone on the team can always follow the process.

### Problems and Things to Think About

### Cost of Infrastructure

Keeping two settings exactly the same, even if one isn't being used much, can add to the cost of infrastructure. Companies need to weigh the costs of less downtime and higher dependability against the benefits they bring.

### Moving data around

It can be hard to manage data migration during a Blue/Green release if your app uses databases or other data stores. To make sure that data is always the same, you need to carefully plan and synchronize your systems.

### Session Lasting Power

It can be hard to make sure that applications that depend on session persistence can switch smoothly from Blue to Green settings. It's possible that techniques like "sticky sessions" or centralized session control will be needed.

### Change Control

Keeping track of all the different versions of your app's code can be hard, especially if there are a lot of release cycles. To avoid confusion and disagreements, it's important to use strong version control methods.

When it comes to DevOps and continuous delivery, blue/green deployments are a great way to make sure that software is delivered smoothly. Companies can release new features and updates with no downtime, less risk, and more flexibility if they keep different, fully tested environments and switch between them. The pros of Blue/Green deployments make them a useful tool for current software development teams, even though there are some issues to think about. Using this method can make users happy, speed up releases, and make the ecosystem for apps more stable and reliable.

## 7.2 Canary Releases

Companies are always looking for ways to add new features, updates, or improvements to software without putting users at risk. This is because software creation and deployment are always changing. Canary releases have become a powerful way to find this delicate balance. They let teams make changes slowly while closely watching how they affect a small group of users. We'll talk about what Canary releases are, why they're important, the best ways to use them, and their pros and cons in this piece.

### How to Understand Canary Releases

If you want to test changes on a small group of users or servers before a full release, you can use a method called "canary releases," which is also called "canary deployments" or "canary testing." The word "canary" comes from the use of canaries in coal mines to find dangerous gases. If a canary showed signs of suffering, it meant that there might be a danger. Canary versions are like early warning systems in software development; they help teams find and fix problems before they appear for all users.

### The Phase of the Canary

A small group of people or servers are chosen to get the update or feature that is being rolled out in a canary release. People who use this service, who are sometimes called "canaries," are picked to be typical of all users. During the canary phase, organizations can get feedback and data about the changes in the real world while reducing their exposure to possible problems.

Rollout over time

The organization keeps a close eye on the canaries' experiences once they are introduced to the new code or configuration. Performance metrics, error rates, user feedback, and other important data points are all part of this monitoring. The organization gradually expands the rollout percentage to a bigger group of users or computers if no major problems are found.

Alerts and monitoring

Monitoring and reporting all the time are important parts of canary releases. Teams use real-time data and set limits to figure out whether the canary phase should go on, be stopped, or be undone completely. The deployment can be stopped or rolled back if problems are found, so that most users are not harmed.

Canary Releases Pros and Cons

Getting rid of risks

One of the main benefits of canary releases is that they lower danger. Organizations can find and fix problems early by letting a small group of users experience changes first. This stops problems from spreading and lessens the effect on most users. This method makes it less likely that there will be large-scale problems or downtime.

Tests in the Real World

With a canary release, you can test in the real world in a controlled setting. In the canary phase, user feedback, performance metrics, and error rates can give you information that you might not get in a normal testing setting. This information helps companies decide if they want to go ahead with the deployment or not.

Loop that responds faster

A faster feedback loop is made by canary escapes. Instead of waiting for problems to show up after the release, teams get feedback right away from the canaries. This lets changes and iterations happen quickly, which improves the quality of the release as a whole.

Rollout in Small Steps

Changes can be rolled out slowly by organizations, which lets them slowly raise the deployment percentage as trust grows. When it comes to large-scale applications and critical systems, where a sudden failure can have big effects, this gradual method works best.

### Approach Focused on Users

When Canary updates come out, the user experience comes first. Companies show they care about giving their customers a stable and reliable service by keeping a close eye on the canaries and fixing any problems right away.

### The best ways to release a canary

#### Make your goals clear

Set clear goals and success factors before starting a canary release. What do you want this update to do for you? How will you tell if you've been successful or not? You can make better decisions during the canary phase if you have a clear plan.

#### Choose some representative canaries

Pick canaries that show various types of users, their habits, or different use cases. This makes sure that the feedback and data you get in the beta process are representative of all of your users.

#### Watch over and warn

Set up strong tracking and alerting systems to keep an eye on the health and performance of canaries all the time. Set limits for important measures and make sure that alerts go off when those limits are crossed. This kind of proactive tracking is necessary to find problems quickly.

#### Rollout over time

Start with a small number of canaries, usually between 1% and 10%. As you get more confident in the security of the deployment, slowly increase the rollout percentage. At every stage of the spread, keep a close eye on things.

#### Plan to Go Back

Make sure you have a clear plan for rolling back changes. You should be ready to undo the changes if problems appear during the canary phase that can't be fixed quickly. This will make sure that users are affected as little as possible.

#### Express Yourself Clearly

Keep the lines of contact open with the canaries and the rest of the users. Users should be told that they are part of a beta update and be asked to give feedback. Being open and honest helps people believe you and understand how the deployment works.

### Problems and Things to Think About

#### Choose the Canary

It can be hard to choose canaries that truly represent your users. If you don't pick the right canaries, the info and feedback you get might be wrong.

#### Data Safety

Make sure that the data that is collected during the "canary" process is kept safe and in line with

privacy laws. Keep the identity of canaries and users who are taking part in the release safe.

Level of difficulty

Keeping track of canary releases can make deployment processes more complicated. Teams need to spend money on technology and tools to make the process go more smoothly.

Needs for Resources

For monitoring and control, canary releases need more resources. During deployments,

organizations should be ready for more resources to be used.

Above head

Managing canary releases and keeping up with various environments can add extra work. Businesses need to compare the pros and cons of their actions.

Canary versions are a good way to get software out there when you want to minimize risk, improve user experience, and get feedback quickly. By letting a small group of users or servers see changes before the full release, companies can find and fix problems early on, which makes the rollout process go more smoothly and gives users a better experience. While there are some problems with canary releases, they are a useful tool for modern software development teams that want to make their goods and services both innovative and reliable.

7.3 Containerization and Orchestration

Today's software development and deployment is very fast-paced. Containerization and orchestration have become revolutionary technologies that have changed how apps are built, shipped, and controlled. Containerization (Docker is the most famous platform) and orchestration tools (Kubernetes) have changed how developers and operations teams work together, make workflows more efficient, and make sure that the system is scalable, available, and reliable. This piece talks about the ideas behind containerization and orchestration as well as their pros, cons, and possible futures.

A paradigm shift in containerization

Containerization is a technology that builds a program and all of its dependencies into a single, small, and stable unit called a container. The application code, runtime, libraries, and dependencies are all contained within these containers. This makes sure that the app runs the same way in all settings. Containerization has become the de facto standard, and Docker made this method famous by making it easy to make, distribute, and run containers.

### Pros of using containers

**Consistency:** Containers make sure that an app works the same way on a developer's laptop, a test server, and a production system. This gets rid of the annoying "it works on my machine" problem.

**Isolation:** Containers are separated from the host system and each other. This keeps apps from fighting with each other and prevents conflicts.

**Portability:** Containers can run on any system that supports the containerization platform. This makes it simple to move apps between cloud providers, data centers, or computers on-premises.

**Resource Efficiency:** Since containers share the OS kernel of the host, they are lighter and use fewer resources than standard virtual machines.

**Rapid Deployment:** Containers can be made and put into use quickly, which allows for continuous integration/continuous deployment (CI/CD) processes and quick development.

**Version Control:** It's easy to go back to earlier versions of containers if something goes wrong because they can be versioned.

**Scalability:** To handle more work, containers can be quickly copied and scaled horizontally.

**Security:** Containers help keep security breaches inside their boundaries, and there are many tools that can be used to check container pictures for holes.

### Managing container ecosystems through orchestration

Containerization makes shipping and packaging easier, but it can be hard to keep track of a lot of containers in a work setting. This is where orchestrating containers comes in. The process of automating the deployment, scaling, control, and monitoring of containers and the apps that run in them is called container orchestration. Kubernetes, which was made by Google, has become the most popular orchestration tool.

### Pros of Using Orchestration

**Automated Scaling:** Orchestration platforms like Kubernetes can automatically scale up or down apps based on traffic and resource needs. This makes sure that resources are used in the best way possible.

**High Availability:** Orchestration makes it possible to ensure high availability, fault tolerance, and emergency recovery, which cuts down on downtime.

**Load Balancing:** Orchestration platforms handle load balancing to spread data evenly across containers, which makes applications run faster and more reliably.

**Self-Healing:** If a container or node fails, orchestration systems can move containers to healthy nodes automatically, which keeps applications running.

**Rolling Updates:** Orchestration makes it possible to update and delete apps without any problems, which lowers the risk of putting out new versions.

**Declarative Configuration:** Kubernetes uses this method. Users tell the platform what state they want the system to be in, and it takes care of getting there. This makes configuration management easier.

**Resource Optimization:** Orchestration systems can make the best use of CPU and memory by optimizing how resources are allocated.

**Ecosystem Integration:** Kubernetes has a large ecosystem of add-ons and integrations, such as tracking, logging, and security tools, which makes it flexible for a wide range of uses.

Containerization and orchestration have some problems.

Containerization and automation have many benefits, but they also come with some problems that businesses need to solve in order to get the most out of them.

Level of difficulty

Managing and managing containers is hard work that needs people who are good at both development and operations. For organizations to use these technologies successfully, they may need to spend money on training and skill development.

Peace of mind

Security for containers is very important. Containers can help keep things separate, but they also make it easier for hackers to get in. Best practices must be used by organizations to protect container files, runtime environments, and orchestration platforms.

Linking up

When you're working with microservices designs, networking in containerized environments can be hard. Orchestrators are in charge of making sure that containers can talk to each other over the network, which often requires complex settings.

Monitoring and being able to see

Because containerized environments change quickly, it is important to be able to watch and see what is going on. To understand how well containers are working and fix problems, organizations need to set up good tracking tools.

Keeping at it

Most containers don't keep any data, which can be a problem for apps that need to keep data. Careful planning is needed to manage stateful containers and make sure that data stays the same.

What's Coming Up

Containers without servers

Serverless technologies are becoming more popular, and people want to find ways to combine the benefits of containers with serverless computing. This trend could lead to more container systems and solutions that don't need a server.

### Using the Edge

A rising trend is edge computing, in which programs run closer to the source of the data. It's possible that orchestration and containers will be used to manage and scale edge apps.

### Better experience for developers

Developers can look forward to better systems and tools for making and testing containers. This will make the process of containerization easier for developers.

### Using Multiple Clouds and Hybrid Systems

Containerization and orchestration will be very important for letting apps run smoothly across various cloud providers and on-premises environments as companies try to avoid being locked into one vendor.

### Better security measures

More advanced tools for finding threats, checking for vulnerabilities, and making sure compliance are added to container security all the time.

## 7.4 Scalability and Performance Considerations

Scalability and performance of software tools are very important in today's digital world. Your ability to handle growing workloads and provide responsive user experiences is key to your success whether you are making a web app, a cloud service, or a business system. This piece will talk about scalability and performance issues, as well as ways to improve both. It will also talk about tools and best practices that can help you make systems that are strong and work well.

### How to Understand Performance and Scalability

### How to Scale

One definition of scalability is a system's ability to handle more work and more users without slowing down. It's about making systems that can grow both up and down (by adding more resources to a single machine) and side to side (by adding more machines to a networked system).

Vertical scalability means giving a single machine more resources like CPU, memory, and storage. A certain amount of this can work, but it has its limits because technology resources have a limit.

Horizontal scalability means adding more tools to a system and dividing the work between them. This method is more environmentally friendly, and it can be made more flexible by adding more tools as needed.

### How it Works

Performance, on the other hand, is how quickly and well a system reacts to user requests and completes tasks. It's about making sure the system works at a good speed and gives users a good experience in all sorts of situations.

Different measures can be used to judge performance, such as:

The amount of time it takes for a request to be handled and an answer to be sent.

This is the number of calls that a system can handle in one unit of time.

Resource Utilization is the measure of how well system resources like CPU, memory, and files are used.

Important Things to Think About for Performance and Scalability

1. Building and design

   Pick the Right Building Style: Pick an architecture that meets the needs of your program. Microservices architectures, on the other hand, are great for horizontal scalability, while monolithic architectures may be easier to handle for small apps.

   Decompose the System: Split your program into smaller parts that are easier to handle. This lets you scale different parts separately and makes it easier to find problems.

2. Balancing the load

   Load Balancers: If you want to evenly spread incoming traffic across multiple instances of your app, you should use load balancers. This keeps each instance from getting too busy, which makes both scalability and speed better.

3. Making a database

   Database Scaling: The database slows things down a lot of the time. To deal with growing amounts of data, you might want to use database replication, sharding, or NoSQL systems.

   Caching: To make database loads lighter and reaction times faster, use caching mechanisms. Redis and Memcached are two well-known caching options.

4. Code That Works

   Optimize Code: Write code and methods that work well. Profile and optimize important parts of your application on a regular basis to lower resource use and boost speed.

   Asynchronous Processing: For jobs that don't need answers right away, use asynchronous processing. This can free up the main thread of the program and make it faster.

5. Tracking and making profiles

   Monitoring Tools: Set up strong monitoring and warning systems to learn more about how systems work. For this, people often use tools like Prometheus and Grafana.

   Profiling: To find places in your code and systems that slow things

down, use profiling tools. Profilers, such as the Java VisualVM and Python's cProfile, can help you find places where you can improve.
6. Infrastructure that can grow
   Cloud Services: Use cloud services that can automatically scale, such as AWS, Azure, or Google Cloud. Based on demand, these systems can automatically add and remove resources.
   Organization and Containerization: To handle and grow your apps effectively, use organization and containerization platforms (like Docker) and tools (like Kubernetes).
7. Delivery of Content
   Content Delivery Networks (CDNs): CDNs can be used to get static files closer to users, which lowers latency and speeds up load times.
8. Safety
   Measures for Security: Use security techniques that don't slow down work. This includes making sure that security steps like encryption and authentication don't add a lot of extra work.
9. Comparisons and tests

Load Testing: You should test your app's behavior under a lot of stress by doing load testing. Apache JMeter and Gatling are two tools that can help you model situations with a lot of traffic.

Benchmarking: Track and compare the success of your app on a regular basis with set goals and industry standards.

Examples from real life

1. Netflix
   Netflix is a big name in streaming, and it uses tools like Apache Cassandra and Apache Kafka to make its systems grow horizontally. They also put a lot of money into delivering content and use adaptable streaming algorithms to make sure users can play content smoothly.
2. Search Engine
   People know that Google's search engine responds very quickly. Google does this with the help of caching, distributed computers, and complex algorithms that decide which search results to show first.
3. HomeAway

Airbnb is a platform that handles a huge amount of user-generated content. To make sure that property listings load quickly and consistently for users all over the world, the company uses both sharding and caching.

Performance and scalability are important parts of both making software and designing systems. To make systems that work well and are reliable, you need to think carefully about architectural choices, code efficiency, infrastructure choices, and how to watch systems. By following best practices and always making your app better, you can give your users great experiences and keep up with growing workloads. This will keep your software competitive and reliable in a digital world that is changing quickly. Keep in mind that speed and scalability are ongoing issues that need to be fixed and improved as your application changes and user needs shift.

# Chapter 8

## Security in Cloud-Based CI/CD

With the rise of cloud computers, the way software is made and used has changed. CI/CD systems, which stand for Continuous Integration and Continuous Deployment, are now necessary for getting software out quickly and reliably. But moving to cloud-based CI/CD also brings new security issues and things that companies need to think about in order to keep their code, infrastructure, and private data safe. This guide will go over everything you need to know about security in cloud-based CI/CD. We will look at risks, best practices, and tools that can protect the whole development and delivery process.

**The Beginning**

Continuous Integration and Continuous Deployment (CI/CD) in the cloud have changed the way software is made by making software release faster and more reliable. This method automates the process of creating, testing, and launching apps, which cuts down on manual work and speeds up the time it takes to get products to market. There are, however, new security issues and concerns that come up with cloud-based CI/CD.

The purpose of this piece is to talk about how important security is in cloud-based CI/CD pipelines, the threats that could happen, and the best ways to keep your code and infrastructure safe during the development and delivery process.

**Risks to Security in CI/CD in the Cloud**

To keep a cloud-based CI/CD pipeline safe, you need to deal with a number of risks that can damage the pipeline, steal your code, or make your services unavailable.

1. **Access Without Permission**

    Attackers can get into your CI/CD tools, repositories, or systems and use them without your permission. This could cause private data to be stolen, data breaches, or code changes.

2. Injection of code

   If you don't properly clean your pipeline, code injection attacks like SQL injection or remote code execution can get in and damage it. Attackers can use holes in your code, scripts, or setup files to do harm.

3. Dependencies that aren't safe

   A lot of software projects depend on libraries and files made by other people. An attacker could use these dependencies to get into your system if they have security holes.

4. Not enough authorization and authentication

   If your authentication and permission systems aren't strong enough, people who aren't supposed to be there can get into your CI/CD tools, change code, or do other illegal things.

5. Configuration that isn't safe

   If you don't set up CI/CD tools, cloud services, or containers correctly, they could leave private data open or give too many permissions, which would leave your pipeline open to attacks.

6. Breach of Data

   If you don't protect your CI/CD pipeline well, sensitive data like API keys, passwords, or customer information could be made public.

7. Attacks by DDoS

   Distributed Denial of Service (DDoS) attacks can make your CI/CD pipeline unavailable by sending too much data to it.

8. Threats from inside

Insiders who are malicious or not careful can be a big security risk to your CI/CD process because they may be able to get to important systems and data.

The safest ways to use cloud-based CI/CD

To protect their cloud-based CI/CD systems from the above security threats, businesses should follow a set of best practices.

1. Management of identities and access

   Make sure that only authorized people and services can get into your CI/CD tools and infrastructure by putting in place strong identification and access management controls.

2. Signing code

   Digitally sign your code to make sure it is real and correct during the CI/CD process. This stops other people from running the code without your permission.

3. **Keep dependencies safe**
Dependencies should be updated and patched regularly to fix known security holes. Use tools for security screening to find and fix parts that are weak.

4. **Safety for Infrastructure as Code (IaC)**
Use security best practices for your Infrastructure as Code templates to keep cloud resources safe and avoid mistakes in setup.

5. **Secret codes**
When data is at rest and when it is being sent, encrypt it. Make sure that secrets, settings, and messages sent between CI/CD components are encrypted.

6. **Monitoring all the time**
Your CI/CD process should be constantly checked and monitored so that you can find and fix security problems as they happen.

7. **The principle of least privilege**
Make sure that users and services only have the rights they need to do their jobs by following the principle of least privilege.

8. **Cloud DevOps**
DevSecOps says that you should build security into your CI/CD process from the start. As part of your CI/CD process, test for security, look over the code, and look for holes.

9. **Back-ups and disaster recovery**
Make sure your CI/CD pipeline is always available by setting up emergency recovery plans and multiple copies of it.

10. **Training and knowledge about security**

Teach your operations and development teams about good security techniques and how important it is to have security in the CI/CD process.

**Tools and technologies for security**

1. **Scanning for security in containers**
Clair, Trivy, and Anchore are some of the tools that can check container images for security holes. This makes sure that only safe containers are released.

2. **Management of security information and events**
SIEM tools, such as Splunk or ELK Stack, can keep an eye on your CI/CD pipeline in real time and let you know about any security issues that happen.

3. Firewalls that protect web apps
   Your web apps can be safe from code injection and other threats with WAFs like ModSecurity or AWS WAF.
4. Dealing with secrets
   You can keep secrets used in your CI/CD process safe and change them regularly with tools like
   HashiCorp Vault or AWS Secrets Manager.
5. Looking at and scanning code
   Tools for Static Application Security Testing (SAST) and Dynamic Application Security Testing (DAST) can help find weak spots and holes in code.
6. Scanning for security in infrastructure as code (IaC)
   IaC files can be checked for security holes by tools like Checkov or AWS Config.
7. MFA stands for "multi-factor authentication."

To make things even safer, require multifactor authentication (MFA) for CI/CD tools and important platforms.

Thoughts on Compliance and Regulation

1. GDPR
   If you deal with personal information of people in the European Union (EU), make sure you follow the General Data Protection Regulation (GDPR), which sets rules for privacy and protecting data.
2. The HIPAA
   Healthcare groups that deal with patient information must follow the Health Insurance Portability and Accountability Act (HIPAA) rules, which require strict security measures.
3. The PCI DSS
   Companies that take credit card payments must follow the Payment Card Industry Data Security Standard (PCI DSS).
4. SOC 2
   Service Organization Control (SOC 2) compliance makes sure that companies follow rules for security, availability, handling integrity, privacy, and keeping information secret.
5. ISO 27001

ISO 27001 is a well-known standard for information security management systems (ISMS) that can be very important for companies that care a lot about security.

Education and Culture of Security

It is very important to make your organization's mindset security-conscious. Employees can understand what they need to do to keep the CI/CD system safe through regular training and awareness programs. Encourage people to report security problems right away, and give rewards to people who do so.

## 8.1 Security Challenges in CI/CD Pipelines

CI/CD pipelines, which stand for Continuous Integration and Continuous Deployment, are essential to modern software development. They help companies release software more quickly and accurately. But while CI/CD pipelines make the development and deployment processes faster and easier, they also bring new security issues that companies need to deal with to keep their code, data, and systems safe. We will look at the security problems that CI/CD pipelines face and talk about ways to fix them in this piece.

### Getting to Know CI/CD Pipelines

CI/CD pipelines are a set of methods and tools that make the whole process of delivering software automatic, from making changes to the code to putting it into production. Code integration, testing, building, deployment, and monitoring are some of the steps that make up the process. CI is all about automating the testing and integration of changes to code, and CD is all about automating the transfer and deployment of those changes to production.

### Problems with security in CI/CD pipelines

1. **Weak spots in the code**
   Problem: Developers might add SQL injection, cross-site scripting (XSS), or unsafe variables to the codebase, which could make it less secure. Attackers can use these holes during the CI/CD process or after the app has been released.
   Fix: Use security scans and static code analysis tools to find holes in the code early on in the development process. Add security checks to the CI/CD process to keep code that isn't safe from getting released.

2. **Dealing with secrets**
   Problem: CI/CD processes need to be able to access private data like API keys, passwords, and certificates all the time. It can be hard to keep these secrets safe, especially when more than one person on the team has access to them.
   To protect private information, use a secrets management system to store and get it safely. Set up access limits and make sure that secrets aren't shown in configuration files or build logs.

3. Safety of Containers

   Problem: In CI/CD pipelines, containers are often used to package services and apps. But container pictures can pose security risks if they are not properly locked down.

   To fix the problem, use tools like Clair, Trivy, or Anchore to look through container pictures for holes. Make sure that security holes are fixed by regularly updating and patching container files.

4. Orchestration of safety

   Challenge: To keep track of containers and deployments, CI/CD processes often use orchestration tools like Kubernetes or Docker Swarm. Concerns about setup, access control, and network security come up because of these tools.

   Fix: Make sure that the right people can access the orchestration systems. Check settings on a regular basis to make sure they follow best practices for security. To separate CI/CD settings, use network segmentation.

5. Taking care of dependencies

   Problem: Modern apps depend on tools and dependencies from other companies. To fix security holes, it's important to keep these variables up to date and managed.

   Solution: Use tools for dependency scanning to find and fix relationships that are weak. Set up a way to keep track of variables and regularly update them.

6. Safety of Pipelines

   The CI/CD system itself can be attacked, which is a challenge. If you break into the pipeline, bad code could be injected into the program.
   Fix: Make sure the CI/CD pipeline has strong authentication and access rules. Use secure signing tools to make sure that the code is correct throughout the process.

7. Keeping data safe

   The problem is that CI/CD systems might deal with private data like intellectual property or customer data. If the right security steps aren't in place, data breaches can happen.

   As a safety measure, encrypt private data while it's in the pipeline and while it's at rest. Use safe

   ways to store your data and make sure that only authorized people can view it.

8. Rules and regulations that must be followed

Problem: Different industries and areas have different privacy and data security rules and regulations that must be followed. It can be hard to meet these standards.

To avoid problems, learn about the rules and standards that need to be followed, like GDPR, HIPAA, or PCI DSS, and make sure that the CI/CD process matches the right controls and procedures.

Tips for Making the CI/CD Pipeline More Secure

1. Press the left shift key
   Move security techniques from later in the development process to earlier in the software development lifecycle. This means adding security checks and testing right away. During the coding and code review steps, developers should be able to find and fix security problems.
2. Automating
   In the CI/CD process, test and check for security automatically. This includes things like static code analysis, checking for security holes, and testing for security holes automatically. With automated security testing, every change to the code is checked for security problems.
3. Monitoring all the time
   Set up alerts and continuous tracking for the CI/CD pipeline and all of its parts. Security mishaps and strange behavior should be found and fixed right away. Monitoring helps make sure that security stays a top concern all the way through the pipeline.
4. Safety with Code
   Security settings and rules should be thought of as code. To set up and enforce security settings regularly across environments, use Infrastructure as Code (IaC) and policy as code tools.
5. Structures that can't be changed
   You might want to use an immutable infrastructure method, in which infrastructure parts are replaced instead of patched. This lowers the chance of design drift and makes sure that only safe parts are put in place.
6. Going to school and training
   Spend money to teach and train the development and management teams about security. Developers who know about security are more likely to write safe code and follow best practices.
7. Working together
   Encourage the development, management, and security teams to work together. Security should be a big part of DevOps, and teams should work together to fix problems with security.

8. Testing and auditing done regularly

The CI/CD pipeline and all of its parts should have regular security checks and attack tests. Through proactive testing, you can find weak spots and flaws.

To keep software applications safe, private, and accessible, it is important to protect CI/CD processes. As businesses depend more on automated delivery pipelines, the security issues that come up in these pipelines need to be fully addressed.

By learning about the unique security issues that come up in CI/CD pipelines and using techniques like shifting left security, automation, continuous monitoring, and teamwork, businesses can create strong and safe pipelines that allow for quick and reliable software delivery while lowering security risks.

## 8.2 Implementing Security Scans and Checks

It's very important to do full security checks and scans when working with computers these days, because of all the online threats out there. Cybercriminals are always trying to find holes in software and systems and use them to attack businesses all over the world. It's important to build security scans and checks into your development and operational processes to protect against these threats. This article will talk about the importance of security scans and checks, the different kinds and tools that are available, and the best ways to use them successfully.

Why security scans and checks are important

**Identification of Vulnerabilities:** Security scans and checks help find software and system weaknesses, vulnerabilities, or incorrect settings that attackers could use.

**Making Sure Compliance:** They make sure that software and systems follow security rules, laws, and company policies. This lowers the chance of not following the rules and the fines that come with it.

**Data Breach Prevention:** Scan and check tools help protect private data and stop data breaches by finding and fixing security holes.

**Boosting Trust:** Taking proactive security steps can help a business's reputation, which in turn boosts trust among customers, partners, and other important people.

Different kinds of checks and scans for security

1. Checking for Vulnerabilities

    Automated tools that look for known security holes in software, networks, and systems are used for vulnerability testing. It usually checks for things like out-of-date software, wrong settings, and common security problems. A lot of people use tools like Nessus, OpenVAS, and Qualys to look for security holes.

2. **Testing for holes**
Ethical hacking, also known as penetration testing, goes beyond automatic scans by making systems vulnerable to attacks that would happen in real life. Skilled testers try to take advantage of weaknesses in the system to figure out how secure it is. This kind of testing helps you learn more about weaknesses and how they might affect your system.

3. **Review of the code and static analysis**
Reviewing the source code of programs for security holes like SQL injection, cross-site scripting (XSS), and buffer overflows is what code review and static analysis are all about. Automated code analysis tools such as Checkmarx, Fortify, and Veracode help writers find and fix security holes.

4. **Testing the security of dynamic applications**
DAST tools look at programs from the outside, acting out attacks just like a thief would. They find weaknesses by interacting with apps that are already running and looking at how they respond. For DAST, people often use tools like OWASP ZAP and Burp Suite.

5. **Scanning for security in containers**
The main goal of container security scans is to find security holes and threats in containerized apps. They look for known security holes in container files and the libraries they depend on. For protecting containers, many people like to use tools like Clair, Trivy, and Anchore.

6. **Checks for compliance**
Compliance checks make sure that systems and apps follow rules and laws specific to their industry, like PCI DSS, HIPAA, or GDPR. To check for compliance, automated tools and exams are used.

7. **Scanning the network**

Network scanning tools find routers, switches, and firewalls that have open ports, security holes, or are not set up correctly. This helps businesses make their networks safer.

How to Use Security Checks and Scans Correctly

1. **Make your goals clear.**
First, make a list of the exact goals and aims of your security scans and checks. Figure out the scope of your assessments, such as what

assets (like systems, networks, and apps) will be looked at and how often they will be done.

2. **Choose the Right Tools**
   Based on your goals and the types of security holes you want to find, pick the right tools for your security checks. Think about things like how easy it is to use, how scalable it is, and how well it can work with your current systems.

3. **Use automation when you can**
   Use technology to make checks and scans for security easier. Large codebases, networks, and systems can be quickly scanned by automated tools, which makes sure that everything is covered and results are delivered on time.

4. **Connect to CI/CD pipelines**
   Add security checks and scans to your Continuous Integration (CI) and Continuous Deployment (CD) processes. This makes sure that security checks are done automatically at all stages of development and release.

5. **Set up clear steps to follow**
   Set up clear ways to deal with security issues and weaknesses. Set up a way to sort weaknesses into groups based on how bad they are and how they affect the system, and then prioritize fixing them based on those groups.

6. **Get cross-functional teams involved**
   Everyone is responsible for security. Include teams from different departments, such as coders, operations, and security experts, in the process of assessing and fixing problems. Working together makes sure that weaknesses are fixed properly.

7. **Update and patch often**
   It's important to keep your software, systems, and dependencies up to date with security fixes and updates. Patches that fix known security holes should be applied regularly.

8. **Teach and educate staff**
   Your development and operations teams should get security training and programs to raise their knowledge. Staff members who have been trained are better able to spot and fix security problems.

9. **Keep an eye on and check**
   You can find and fix security problems right away if you keep an eye on and check your systems and apps all the time. Review and audit security rules and settings on a regular basis.

10. **Write down and report**

Keep detailed records of security assessments, findings, and attempts to fix problems. Tell the right people about your protection situation and any changes you've made.

Problems and Things to Think About

1. Red Flags and False Positives
   Security tools can give either false positives (finding problems when they don't exist) or false negatives (not finding real flaws). Before taking action, it's important to confirm and evaluate the results.
2. Limitations on Resources
   It takes time, money, and knowledge to do thorough security reviews. Organizations need to make sure they have enough resources to do security checks and scans properly.
3. Changing Nature of Threats
   The threat environment is always changing, with new attack vectors and weaknesses showing up all the time. Businesses need to keep up with new information and change their security steps to match.
4. Privacy and following the law

Following the rules that apply to your business and keeping users' privacy safe are very important things to think about. It is up to organizations to make sure that their security reviews meet these needs.

Checks and scans for security are important parts of a strong cybersecurity plan. Organizations can keep their systems, apps, and data safe from online threats by finding weak spots, making sure they follow the rules, and lowering risks before they happen. For security scans and checks to work well, companies should set clear goals, choose the right tools, automate tasks, involve cross-functional teams, and set priorities for fixing problems. A proactive approach to security is key to keeping people trusting you and protecting your valuable assets in a world where threats are always changing.

8.3 Compliance and Governance

Compliance and control are very important for keeping things in order, making sure people are held accountable, and building trust in a world where business and technology are always changing. These ideas aren't just trendy phrases; they're important parts of how businesses, governments, and groups reach their goals while following the law and doing the right thing. We will learn about compliance and governance, talk about how important they are, and look at the best ways to put them into practice in this piece.

How to Understand Governance and Compliance

Getting Along

Compliance means following the rules, laws, standards, and internal policies that a company has set up for how it works. These can include a lot of different things, like financial rules, data security laws, environmental rules, standards for certain industries, and more.

The goal of compliance activities is to make sure that businesses follow the law and do the right thing. Not following the rules can lead to legal problems, damage to your image, and fines. Compliance is a way for a company to protect itself from bad behavior and misconduct.

Taking charge

Governance, on the other hand, is made up of the rules, methods, and procedures that help people make decisions and keep an eye on things in a company. It includes the rules and procedures that tell you how an organization works, makes choices, and stays responsible.

Governance is more than just following the law and regulations. It includes more than just that. It includes things like strategy planning, risk management, openness, and involving stakeholders. Good governance encourages people to make smart decisions, handle risks, and help the business reach its goals.

Why compliance and governance are important

1. Following the law and rules

    Compliance is the process of making sure that businesses follow the rules. Regulatory groups set rules and standards to protect people, businesses, and the environment, among other things. Compliance helps businesses stay out of trouble with the law and escape fines and other punishments.

2. Taking care of risks

    Risk management plans that find, evaluate, and lower possible risks are an important part of good government. This proactive method helps businesses avoid crises and other problems that come up out of the blue that could stop operations.

3. Doing the right thing

    Compliance and governance systems encourage people to act in an ethical way and make smart decisions. They make an organization's atmosphere one of honesty, integrity, and responsibility.

4. A stable economy

    For keeping finances stable and clear, it's important to have good governance practices, such as financial controls and reports. This is very important for companies that are sold on the stock market and groups that handle public money.

5. **Dealing with Reputation**
   Compliance and governance are both important to the image of a business. Following morals and the law builds trust among users, partners, and investors, among other people.
6. **Trust from Stakeholders**

Good governance systems make sure that companies think about the needs of all stakeholders, like workers, shareholders, customers, and the community. This makes these groups feel more confident and helps them.

The best ways to put compliance and governance into action

1. **Make sure your rules and instructions are clear.**
   Make detailed rules and instructions that spell out what needs to be done to follow the rules and the basic principles of good government. Make sure that your workers can read and understand these documents.
2. **Audits and evaluations of compliance**
   Do compliance checks and assessments on a regular basis to find holes and weak spots. By doing these evaluations, groups can deal with problems before they get too big.
3. **Watch over the board**
   Boards of directors are very important to how things are run. They should be involved in keeping an eye on governance and safety efforts and hold leadership responsible.
4. **School and training**
   Give your workers, management, and other important people in your business training and educational programs to help them learn about and understand compliance and governance requirements.
5. **Taking care of risks**
   Use risk management techniques to find possible dangers, figure out how bad they could be, and come up with ways to lower them. Look over and update risk ratings on a regular basis.
6. **Reporting and being open**
   Keep financial reporting and processes open and honest. To keep people updated, you should put out annual reports, financial statements, and compliance reports.
7. **Programs for "whistleblowers"**
   Set up programs that let workers and other stakeholders report unethical or illegal behavior without fear of retaliation. Keep people who blow the whistle from getting hurt.

8. Constantly getting better
    Review and make changes to compliance and governance systems on a regular basis. Changes in rules, business standards, and best practices should be taken into account.
9. ESG and Green Building

When making your governance framework, you should think about Environmental, Social, and Governance (ESG) issues. Investors and other important people are paying more attention to how sustainable a company is.

Problems and Things to Think About

1. How hard it is
    Regulations can be hard to understand because they change by business, region, and jurisdiction. It can be hard to find your way around all of this complexity, especially for global companies.
2. Limitations on Resources
    It's possible that smaller businesses don't have the means or knowledge to set up strong compliance and governance frameworks. It might be necessary to hire outside help or get advice from experts.
3. Being unwilling to change
    When new compliance and governance practices are put in place, workers and leaders may not want to follow them because they see them as too bureaucratic or too much work. To get past this reluctance, we need to communicate and teach effectively.
4. Changes in the rules
    Laws can change, so businesses need to stay up to date and change how they do things to reflect that. Compliance holes can happen if you don't do this.
5. Privacy of Data

Data privacy laws, like GDPR and CCPA, tell businesses they need to keep customer data safe and let people know how they gather it. It can be hard to make sure that these rules are followed.

Compliance and control are not just formalities; they are important parts of running a business in a way that is responsible and lasts. They protect businesses from legal, financial, and social harm while encouraging honest and ethical behavior. To make compliance and governance work well, people need to be committed, keep evaluating, and be able to change with the laws and rules that are always being made. Organizations can build trust, improve their image, and do well in a competitive global market by putting compliance and governance at the top of their list of priorities.

### 8.4 Secrets Management and Access Control

Today's digital world is full of data breaches and cyber dangers, so keeping secrets safe and controlling who can see them is very important. Organizations deal with a lot of private data, such as API keys, encryption keys, passwords, and other secrets that could be very bad if they were leaked. This piece will talk about secrets management and access control, what they mean, and the best ways to keep private data safe.

**Getting to Know Secrets Management**

Credentials include program, database, service, and account usernames and passwords.

API Keys are the authentication tokens and keys that you use to connect to outside services, APIs, or cloud tools.

Keys that are used to encrypt and decrypt data to keep it safe while it is being sent or stored.

**Tokens:** These include session tokens, access tokens, and restart tokens. They are used for authentication and authorization.

The protection, privacy, and integrity of sensitive data must be maintained through good secrets management. It makes sure that these secrets can only be seen and used by authorized systems and users. This lowers the risk of data leaks and unauthorized access.

**How Important It Is to Keep Secrets**

1. Safety and protection of data

   Most of the time, cyberattacks are aimed at sensitive data like encryption keys and login passwords. Managing secrets well keeps this information safe from people who shouldn't have access to it and from being misused. This lowers the risk of data leaks.

2. Requirements for Compliance

   Protecting sensitive data is required by many businesses and regulatory bodies with strict rules. Managing secrets is important for making sure that rules like GDPR, HIPAA, PCI DSS, and others are followed.

3. The efficiency of operations

   Centralized handling of secrets makes it easier to change, revoke, and check on secrets. This makes operations run more smoothly and lowers the chance of mistakes that come with managing secrets by hand.

4. Trust and a good name

   Customers, partners, and other stakeholders will trust you more if

you keep private information safe. A data breach caused by bad management of secrets can do a lot of damage to a company's image.
5. Practices for cloud-native and devops

Secrets management is important for keeping setup settings safe, connecting microservices, and managing containerized apps in cloud-native and DevOps environments.
What are the best ways to keep secrets?

1. A central place to store secrets
   You should set up a central place to store information, like a vault. Secrets can be kept safe and easily accessed with tools like HashiCorp Vault, AWS Secrets Manager, and Azure Key Vault.
2. Encryption at Rest and While Sent
   Make sure that secrets are encrypted both when they are being stored and when they are being sent. To keep private information safe, use strong encryption methods and protocols.
3. Access Control Based on Roles (RBAC)
   You can control who can see secrets and what they can do by using RBAC. Based on job duties, give people roles and rights.
4. Checks and audits
   Allow tracking and monitoring to keep track of who has access to secrets and find activities that seem fishy. Logs and alerts for security events should be looked at often.
5. Rotation of Secrets
   Set up a strategy for rotating secrets to keep credentials and keys up to date. Automated spinning lowers the chance of having secrets exposed for a long time.
6. Versioning Secrets
   Use versioning for secrets to keep track of past information. This lets you go back in time in case of mistakes or security breaches.
7. Injection of Secrets
   Use safe ways to connect managing secrets to applications and infrastructure. Don't put secrets in code or settings files that can't be changed.
8. Use safe building methods

Teach coders how to code safely, and stress how important it is to keep secrets safe. Use code-scanning tools to find and fix security holes that could expose secrets.
How Access Control Works

Setting up and following rules and policies about who can access what resources in an organization's systems and infrastructure is what access control is all about. Access control methods make sure that only people, processes, or systems that are allowed to can get to certain services, data, or resources.

1. Using role-based access control (RBAC), users are given roles, and the rights that come with those roles. Users get the permissions that come with their jobs.
2. **Attribute-Based Access Control (ABAC):** This type of access control decides who can see what based on things like the user's department and job title, the resource's security level, and the time of day.
3. The person who owns the resource decides who can access it and how they can control access. This is called discretionary access control (DAC).
4. **Mandatory Access Control (MAC):** Security marks and classification levels are used to decide who can access a building. These are often used in government and military settings.
5. **Role-Based Access Control (RBAC):** The system gives users roles and the rights that come with them. Users get the permissions that come with their jobs.

Why access control is important

1. Keeping data safe
   Access control keeps people who aren't supposed to be there from getting to private data and stealing, changing, or destroying it.
2. How to Keep Things Private and Secret
   Access control makes sure that data is kept private and secure by only letting authorized people see it.
3. Requirements for Compliance
   A lot of rules, like GDPR, HIPAA, and SOX, say that businesses need to put in place access controls to keep private information safe and make sure they follow the rules.
4. Taking care of risks
   Access control lowers the risk of data breaches and other illegal activities, which helps businesses handle their risks.
5. The efficiency of operations

It is easier to handle user access, permissions, and privileges when access control makes it easier to divide up resources. This makes operations run more smoothly and lowers the chance of mistakes.

The best ways to control access

1. The principle of least privilege
   Give users and processes only the rights they need to do their jobs by following the principle of least privilege. Avoid accounts with too many privileges.
2. Audits and reviews of access
   Review and check users' entry rights and permissions on a regular basis. Quickly remove any entry rights that aren't needed or are out of date.
3. Strong Proof of Identity
   Use strong authentication methods, like multi-factor authentication (MFA), to make sure that
   people and systems are who they say they are.
4. ACLs, or Access Control Lists
   You can tell people who can see certain tools or data by using access control lists. ACLs give
   you fine-grained control over who can view what.
5. Proper training and education
   Teach users and workers why access control and security are important. Encourage a community that cares about security.
6. Identity and Access Management (IAM) that is centralized
   Set up centralized identity and access management (IAM) solutions to control user identities, access, and authentication across all apps and systems.
7. Monitoring all the time

Keep an eye on what users are doing and how they are trying to get in all the time. Find and stop any strange or illegal activity happening right now.

Problems and Things to Think About

1. How hard it is
   It can be hard to keep track of a lot of secrets and access rules, especially in companies with a lot of different systems and apps.
2. Convenience for users vs. safety
   It can be hard to find a good balance between user ease and security.

Users may not like stricter access controls, but security may be compromised by less strict controls.
3. Requirements for Compliance
   Meeting compliance standards like GDPR and HIPAA can take a lot of time and money because they require a lot of paperwork and audits.
4. Integration of a Third Party
   It might not be easy to combine managing codes and controlling access with cloud providers, external apps, and third-party services.
5. Threats that are new

New attack vectors and security holes appear all the time, so the threat environment is always changing. This means that organizations need to change how they protect data.

Access control and managing secrets well are important parts of a strong cybersecurity plan. They keep private data safe, make sure rules are followed, protect secret information, and lower the risk of security breaches. Companies can make their defenses stronger and keep the trust of their customers, partners, and other important people in a world that is becoming more and more digital by following best practices, keeping an eye out for new threats, and encouraging a culture of security awareness.

# Chapter 9

Best Practices and Tips

In today's fast-paced world, people in all areas and industries want to be successful. Adopting best practices and using useful tips can greatly increase your chances of reaching your goals, whether you're a student trying to do well in school, an entrepreneur trying to grow your business, or a professional trying to move up in your job. This complete guide looks at the best ways to do things to do well in many areas of life and work, including personal growth, business success, school, and more.

1. Developing yourself
   Setting Goals
   Personal growth starts with making goals that are clear and attainable. Set both short-term and long-term goals, and make sure they are clear, measured, and have due dates (SMART goals). To stay on track, look at your goals often and make any necessary changes.
   Managing your time
   Managing your time well is an important part of growing as a person. Set priorities, make plans, and cut down on distractions as much as possible. To-do lists and tools that track your time can help you stay on top of things.
   Learning All the Time
   Do not stop learning. Read books, take online classes, go to conferences, and attend workshops to improve yourself. Learn new things and get new skills to stay useful and flexible in a world that changes quickly.
   Taking care of yourself
   To be successful, you need to take care of your physical and mental health. A balanced diet, regular exercise, and enough sleep are all

important parts of a healthy living. To deal with the problems that come up in life, practice awareness and ways to deal with stress.

**Linking up**

Grow and take care of a strong business network. Go to events in your field, join groups that are related, and interact on social media sites. Meeting new people and making useful links can happen through networking.

2. **Learning**

   **Learn by Doing**

   Take an active role in your education by taking part in class talks, asking questions, and getting more information when you need it. Active learning helps you remember things and encourages you to think critically.

   **Tips for Studying**

   Try out different ways to study to see which one works best for you. This could mean making flashcards, mind maps, summarizing notes, or teaching someone else the subject.

   **Managing your time**

   Students need to be able to handle their time well. Set aside time to study each subject on your plan and stick to it. Don't put things off, and make good use of breaks to relax and recharge.

   **Get help**

   If you're having trouble with a subject, don't be afraid to ask for help. Talk to your teachers, tutors, or peers. There are also a lot of online tools and tutoring services that you can use.

   **Stay interested**

   Develop an interest in things. Read a lot, take part in conversations, and learn about things that aren't in your curriculum. A desire to learn that lasts a lifetime comes from being curious.

3. **Getting ahead in your career and profession**

   **Make your job goals clear**

   Write down your job aspirations and goals. List the abilities, credentials, and work experience you'll need to reach your goals. As your job goes on, you should go back and change your career plan often.

   **Linking up**

   In the business world, networking is just as important. Go to workshops, seminars, and events in your field. Connect with coworkers on LinkedIn and keep in touch with teachers and peers in a meaningful way.

   **Getting Better Skills**

   Keep improving your skills to stay ahead of the competition. Use workshops, training programs, and online courses to your benefit.

Keep up with the latest tools and trends in your field.

### How to Communicate Well

In any job, being able to communicate clearly is very important. Improve your listening and speaking skills as well as the way you write. Communication that works well helps people work together and understand each other.

### Managing your time

Time management isn't just important for school. You can use it at work by setting deadlines, prioritizing tasks, and making the most of your time. To stay prepared, use tools that help you get things done.

4. Starting a business and making it successful

### Studying the Market

Do a lot of study on the market before you start your business. Know your competition, the people you want to sell to, and the trends in your business. This information is very important for making smart choices.

### Planning a business

Make a well-thought-out business plan that includes your goals, strategies, and purpose. Include marketing plans, cash projections, and a road map for how the business will run. A good plan shows you how to reach your goals.

### Focusing on the customer

Focus on giving your people the best value possible. Pay attention to what they say and change your services or goods based on what they say. Getting to know your customers well is important for long-term success.

### Management of money

Learn how to handle your money well so that your business can last. Keep an eye on your cash flow, make a smart budget, and get help from a professional when you need it. Making smart financial choices is very important.

### Ability to adapt

Things in business are always changing. Be able to change and adapt. Be open to new ideas and ready to change your business plan if you need to. In places that are always changing, staying flexible can help you do well.

5. Health and well-being

### Put your physical health first

Set aside time to exercise regularly and eat a healthy diet. Your mental health and overall productivity are closely linked to your physical health.

### Awareness of Mental Health

Pay attention to mental health. Watch out for signs of worry, anxiety, or depression, and if you need to, get help. Mindfulness and relaxation methods can help you take care of your mental health.

**Good Sleep Habits**

Getting enough sleep is important for both mental and emotional health. Set a regular sleep routine and make your room a good place to sleep.

**Balance between work and life**

To avoid burnout, try to find a good mix between work and life. Separate your work life from your personal life, and make time for hobbies, relaxing, and spending time with people you care about.

**Check-Ups Every Month**

Get regular check-ups with your doctor to find and treat any health problems early on. To stay healthy, it's important to avoid problems and find them early.

6. Taking care of money

**Making a budget**

Making a budget that takes into account your income, spending, and savings goals is important. Don't worry about money; stick to your limit.

**Fund for Emergencies**

Set up an emergency fund to handle costs that come up out of the blue. Having a safety net for your money gives you peace of mind and keeps you from getting into debt.

**Taking care of debt**

Make a plan for how you will pay off your bills if you have any. Put high-interest bills at the top of your list, and think about consolidating your loans to get lower interest rates.

**Planning for investments and retirement**

A good way to get rich over time is to start saving early. Look into things like stocks, bonds, and savings accounts. Talk to a financial advisor about how to build a diverse portfolio of investments.

**Learning about money**

Learn about how to handle your own money. Read books, go to seminars, and keep up with respected money blogs. Knowing about money is important for making smart choices.

To be successful in many areas of your life and at work, you need to use both best practices and useful tips. The ideas in this guide can help you with all of your goals, whether they are personal growth, education, job advancement, starting your own business, health, or managing your money. Don't forget that success is a journey and that the only way to meet your goals is to keep getting better. You can make your future better and more rewarding by following these best practices and tips.

## 9.1 Lessons Learned from Successful Implementations

Implementations that work well are the result of careful planning, hard work, and the ability to change. It doesn't matter if it's a new business, a software rollout, a community project, or a personal project; learning from successful efforts can help with future projects. In this look at what we can learn from great implementations, we'll look at the main ideas and lessons that have always led to good results.

### Clear goals and a vision

A clear vision and well-defined goals are the first steps to a successful execution. It's important to have a clear idea of what needs to be done before starting a personal project, releasing a new product, or changing the way a company does things. It's easy to lose focus and direction when you don't know what you're trying to do.

Take the time to write down your goals and ideas before you start implementing anything. They should be clear, measurable, attainable, important, and have a due date (SMART). This will be your compass during the whole process.

### All-around Planning

Planning is the most important part of putting things into action. It requires a lot of careful study, figuring out the risks, and coming up with a well-thought-out plan. Planning well, whether it's for a business, a project, or yourself, makes sure you're ready for problems that come up out of the blue.

**Lesson:** Give the planning part enough time and effort. Plan for possible problems that might come up and have backup plans ready. The more carefully you plan, the better you'll be able to handle problems.

### Talking and getting involved

Communication is a key part of any strategy. Clear and useful communication with partners, clients, and team members is a top priority for projects that succeed. Clear goals, regular updates, and active listening are all very important parts of this process.

**Lesson:** Make a strong plan for conversation right away. Make sure that everyone knows what they need to know and is on the same page. Encourage people to give you feedback, and be ready to change based on what they say.

### Allocation of Resources

Allocating resources efficiently is a must for good implementations. It's important to know how to best use resources like money, people, and time so that a project succeeds or fails. Not having enough tools can cause delays and poor results.

**Lesson:** Do a full evaluation of your resources. Use your resources wisely and be ready to change how they are used if necessary. Watch how resources are used during the execution to make sure there aren't any shortages or overages.

### Dealing with Risk

There are risks in every project. Finding possible risks and coming up with ways to reduce them is an important part of a good implementation. This proactive method makes sure you're ready to deal with problems as they come up.

**Lesson:** Make a risk management plan that lists possible dangers, how they might affect you, and what you can do to lower those risks. Review and change this plan often to stay ahead of new risks.

### Adaptability and adaptability

Adaptability is often needed for projects to go well. Situations change and problems appear out of the blue, so it's important to be able to pivot or change your plan. Projects that are adaptable are able to adapt to problems as they come up.

**Lesson:** Be open to change and ready to change your plans when you need to. Keep in mind that you can always do better, and don't let failures get you down. Being able to change is a great success tool.

### Making decisions based on data

Data can help you make choices during an implementation by giving you useful information. Data is used to track progress, measure results, and find places where things could be better. Making decisions based on data improves speed and effectiveness.

**Lesson:** Set up key performance indicators (KPIs) and collect useful data early on in the implementation process. Review and analyze this data on a regular basis to help you make smart choices and push for improvements.

### Sustainability and Planning for the Long Term

Implementations that work well often think about their long-term effects and how they can last. Thinking beyond the short-term benefits of a business plan, a community project, or a personal goal will make sure that the work continues to pay off in the long run.

**Lesson:** Think about what your execution will mean in the long run. Think about what the long-term effects will be on people and the world. You should look for answers that work now and will last for a long time afterward.

### Feedback and evaluation all the time

The process doesn't end when an implementation is deemed good. Continuous review and feedback loops are necessary to keep things going well and make them even better. Ask partners and team members for feedback on a regular basis to find places where things could be better.

Setting up ways for ongoing review and feedback is a lesson. Get people to talk about what went well and what could be done better in an open and honest way. Use this feedback to help with future efforts.

### Happy Holidays and Thanks

It's important to keep up morale and drive by celebrating wins, no matter how small. Recognizing the hard work and commitment of everyone involved makes the atmosphere better and inspires people to do more in the future.

What I learned is that you should celebrate both big and small wins. Recognize what people and teams have done. Parties can boost mood and motivate people to do their best in the future.

Implementations that go well require careful planning, good communication, the ability to change, and a commitment to always getting better. The skills you learn from successful implementations can help you reach your goals, whether you're starting a new business, managing a project, or working toward your own. If you use these lessons and change the way you do things, you'll be better able to deal with problems, take advantage of chances, and finally reach your goals. It's not enough to just get to the end goal; success is also about the trip and the growth that comes with it.

## 9.2 Common Pitfalls to Avoid

People and businesses that want to be successful often face a lot of problems and traps that can slow them down or even cause them to fail. To avoid these common mistakes and stay on track for success, you need to understand and recognize them. This complete guide will look at some of the most common mistakes people make in life, at work, and when making decisions, and give you tips on how to avoid them.

### Not having clear vision and goals

Not having clear goals and vision is one of the biggest problems that people and groups face. It's hard to make good choices and stay focused on important goals when you don't have a clear purpose and direction.

**Strategy to Avoid:** Take the time to make goals that are clear, detailed, and measurable. Create a vision that fits with your goals and ideals. Review and change your goals often to make sure they are still useful.

### Putting things off

People often put things off, which is a bad habit that gets in the way of their progress and efficiency. Putting off important choices and tasks can cause you to miss out on opportunities and feel more stressed.

**Avoidance Strategy:** Learn how to manage your time well, break down big chores into smaller, easier-to-handle steps, and set due dates. To stop putting things off, hold yourself responsible and set priorities.

**Not making plans**

If you don't plan, you're planning to fail. Disorganization, slowness, and bad results can happen when planning isn't done well or at all.

**Avoidance Strategy:** Take the time to plan everything out. Make clear plans of action and methods, and think ahead about what might go wrong. Review your ideas often and make changes as needed.

**Not Talking Enough**

Misunderstandings, fights, and missed chances can happen because of bad communication in both personal and business settings. Not constantly listening or stating your thoughts clearly can slow down progress.

**Avoidance Strategy:** Make good communication a top priority. Pay close attention, speak clearly and briefly, and urge people to talk to each other. Ask for comments often to make your communication better.

**Using up too many resources**

When you spread your resources too thin, like time, money, or people, you can end up with stress, money problems, and poor results.

**Avoidance Strategy:** Be honest about the resources you have access to and wisely distribute them. Be careful not to take on too much, and learn how to say "no" when you need to. Quality should come before number.

**Being unable to adapt**

A big mistake is not being able to change to new situations, technologies, or market conditions. Irrelevance can happen when things don't change.

**Avoidance Strategy:** Be open to change and learn how to adapt. Know what's going on in your field and be open to new tools and ideas. Always be looking for ways to grow and come up with new ideas.

**Not taking care of risk management**

Bad things can happen if you ignore or undervalue possible risks. Problems that come up out of the blue can stop progress and cause loss.

**Avoidance Strategy:** Make a strong plan for dealing with risks. Find possible risks, figure out how bad they could be, and make backup plans. Review and change your risk rating often.

**Try to be perfect**

It can be overwhelming to try to be perfect. It can make you unable to make a choice, criticize yourself too much, and miss important dates.

**Avoidance Strategy:** Strive for quality instead of perfection. Understand that you can't always be perfect and that mistakes are chances to learn and grow. Set guidelines and due dates that are reasonable.

**Managing too closely**

Micromanagement can kill creativity, make workers lose motivation, and slow down work when you're a boss or manager.

**Avoidance Strategy:** Have faith in your team's skills and give them the right tasks and responsibilities. Instead of micromanaging, it's better to set clear goals and offer help.

### Putting Feedback Away

Turning down comments from others, even if it's constructive criticism or useful information, can stop you from growing as a person and as a worker.

**Avoidance Strategy:** Be willing to hear comments and see it as a chance to get better. Ask for feedback from people you trust, and then use that feedback to improve how you do things and the decisions you make.

### Not Delegating Enough

Not willing to give tasks to other people can cause burnout and make it harder for a person or a group to take on bigger challenges.

Deal with the fact that you can't do everything by yourself. Give out tasks based on what each team member is good at. Give clear directions and help when it's needed.

### Thinking in the Present

If you only think about short-term wins or getting what you want right now, you might forget about long-term goals and sustainability.

**Avoidance Strategy:** Think about both the short- and long-term. Put tactics and choices that help you reach your long-term goals and vision at the top of your list.

### Not Enough Self-Care

Self-care that isn't done can cause stress, less work getting done, and worse health.

**Avoidance Strategy:** Put yourself first by taking care of your physical and mental health and relaxing. Set good limits between work and personal life, and ask for help when you need it.

### Not Being Able to Learn from Mistakes

Making the same mistakes over and over again without learning from them can stop you from growing as a person and as a worker.

**Strategy for Avoidance:** Have a growth attitude. Look at your mistakes, figure out why you made them, and use them as chances to get better.

### Not Wanting to Change

Fighting change can slow down growth in both individuals and groups. It can make it hard for people and groups to change and stay important.

**Strategies for Avoidance:** Keep an open mind and see change as a chance to grow. To do well in changing settings, you need to keep learning new things and be able to adapt.

Not only does making the right choices lead to success, but so does avoiding common mistakes that can slow down progress. You can improve your chances of reaching your goals and reaching your full potential by being aware of and avoiding these pitfalls, whether they have to do with making goals, managing your time, communicating, or other areas of your life and work. Remember that avoiding mistakes is an ongoing process that needs you to be self-aware, flexible, and dedicated to always getting better. You can get further on your path to success with more confidence and strength if you avoid these common mistakes.

## 9.3 Tips for Continuous Improvement

Continuous improvement is a basic idea that is essential for personal growth, professional success, and the growth of a company. The goal of excellence by always looking for ways to improve and refine processes, goods, skills, and practices is at the heart of continuous improvement. We will look at a wide range of tips and strategies in this guide that will help you adopt the ideas of continuous improvement and use them in your work and daily life.

**Be clear about your goals and plans.**

Setting clear, specific goals is the first step toward continuous growth. Having a clear picture of what you want to achieve gives your life meaning and purpose, whether it's in your personal or professional life.

**Tip:** Set SMART goals, which stand for Specific, Measurable, Achievable, Relevant, and Time-bound. You can use these goals as a guide to get better.

**Set up a learning culture**

Accept that you will always be learning. Always look for new information, skills, and points of view. Having a learning mindset helps you be flexible and open to change.

**Tip:** Set aside time every week for reading, classes, workshops, or things that help you learn new skills. Get other people in your area to do the same.

**Get information and feedback**

For making smart decisions, you need feedback and facts. Get feedback from customers, peers, or teachers, and collect data to see how far you've come.

**Hint:** To get information, use polls, quizzes, or feedback forms. Look at the data to find patterns and places where things could be better.

**Think and evaluate yourself**

Regularly evaluating yourself is an important part of always getting better. Think about what you did, what you chose, and what happened, and figure out what your strengths and flaws are.

**Tip:** Write down your thoughts and ideas in a diary or use self-evaluation tools. When you judge yourself, be honest and fair.

**Have a growth mindset**

A growth mindset is the idea that you can get smarter and better at things if you work hard and are dedicated. Having this way of thinking gives you the strength to deal with problems and learn from your mistakes.

Tip: When you talk badly to yourself, stop and replace it with positive statements that will help you grow. Recognize failures as chances to learn and get better.

### Time management should come first

Time organization is a very important part of always getting better. It helps you make sure you have time to learn, think, and act.

Tip: To-do lists, calendars, and apps can help you keep track of your time and plan your day so you have time for self-improvement activities.

### Test and come up with new ideas

Experiments and new ideas are often a part of continuous growth. If you want to try something new, don't be afraid to do so.

Tip: Make time for trying new things and coming up with new ideas. Reward people for coming up with new ideas at work to promote a mindset of innovation.

### Actively ask for feedback

Actively asking for feedback from others, like customers, coworkers, or teachers, is a great way to find ways to improve.

Tip: After finishing a job or task, make it a habit to ask for feedback. Allow helpful feedback, and use it to make your skills and methods better.

### Break down big goals.

It can be hard to reach big, complicated goals. To stay motivated and feel like you're making progress, break them up into smaller jobs and goals that you can handle.

TIP: Take the "divide and conquer" method. Make a road map with steps you can take to reach your bigger goals.

### Honor accomplishments

Recognizing and celebrating your successes, no matter how small, is an important way to stay motivated and keep a happy attitude.

Tip: Set goals and give yourself rewards when you meet them. Feel proud and thankful as you celebrate what you've accomplished.

### Learn from your mistakes

In order to get better, you have to be willing to fail sometimes. Instead of seeing it as a loss, see it as a chance to learn something.

Tip: When something goes wrong, you should do a "post-mortem" study to figure out what went wrong and why. Now that you know this, you can avoid making the same mistakes again.

### Stay Up to Date

Do not forget to stay up to date on new technologies, best practices, and business trends. Keeping up with the latest events will keep your skills and information useful.

Tip: Read trade magazines, go to conferences, and join online communities and forums that are related to your area.

**Gather people who can help you.**

Spend time with people who will support and encourage you on your journey to continuous growth. Find mentors and friends who can help you and give you advice.

Tip: Get involved with the people who can help you. Tell them about your problems and goals, and be willing to listen and learn from them.

**Learn to be patient.**

It takes time and patience to work on continuous growth. Results may not come right away, but sticking with it pays off in the end.

Tip: Trust the process and keep your eye on your goals. Don't give in to the urge to hurry or skip steps.

**Review progress often**

To make sure you're on the right track, you need to check in on your success often. They help you figure out what's working and what needs to be changed.

Tip: Schedule time to look over your goals and success every week, month, or three months. Based on what you found, make any changes that are needed.

**When it makes sense, delegate**

Know that you have to ask for help when you need it. When it makes sense, give other people jobs or responsibilities. This lets you concentrate on the places where your skills are most useful.

Tip: Figure out what you're good and bad at and what jobs you can give to other people. When you delegate well, you free up time to work on more important things.

Continuous growth is not a place you get to; it's a way of thinking and a path you take. It means committing to learning new things all your life, reflecting on yourself, being flexible, and always trying to be the best. By using these tips in your work and daily life, you can follow the ideas of continuous growth and do your best in everything you do. Remember that the way to get better is different for everyone, and it takes hard work, patience, and a readiness to accept change. Improving things all the time is a strong force that can lead to success, growth, and new ideas in both personal and business areas.

## 9.4 Future Trends in Cloud-Based CI/CD

Continuous Integration and Continuous Deployment (CI/CD) are important techniques used in modern software development that help teams make high-quality software more quickly and easily. As cloud computing becomes more popular, CI/CD processes are changing to take advantage of the platforms' ability to grow, be flexible, and offer more advanced services. We'll look at the new tools and ways of doing things that are shaping the future of software delivery as we look at future trends in cloud-based CI/CD.

CI/CD without servers

The way software is built and used is changing because of serverless computing. Function as a Service (FaaS) CI/CD, which is another name for serverless CI/CD pipelines, lets developers build, test, and release code without having to worry about the infrastructure underneath. Serverless systems, such as AWS Lambda, Azure Functions, and Google Cloud Functions, make automating CI/CD processes easy, scalable, and cheap.

**Future Effects:** Serverless CI/CD lowers running costs, speeds up deployment, and makes the best use of resources. As serverless systems get better, more people will use them and they will likely be able to work with other CI/CD tools.

Testing Based on Machine Learning

Machine learning (ML) is a big part of making software testing better. Machine learning-based testing tools can make test cases automatically, guess what problems might happen, and even find trends in code changes that could cause bugs.

**Future Effects:** ML-driven testing will make test automation better, cut down on human testing, and raise the quality of software. It will be an important part of CI/CD processes because it gives smart information about the quality of code and test coverage.

Native CI/CD for Kubernetes

It seems like Kubernetes is now the standard way to launch and organize containers. Kubernetes-native CI/CD tools, such as Argo CD and Jenkins X, can directly connect to Kubernetes clusters and make it easier to launch containerized apps.

**Future Effects:** Kubernetes-native CI/CD will continue to grow in popularity as containerization becomes the standard way to package and launch apps. It lets you handle containers efficiently, make them bigger or smaller, and deploy them consistently across environments.

The GitOps

GitOps is a way of doing things that uses Git repositories as the official record for setting up systems and apps. When changes are made to Git, CI/CD pipelines are quickly started. This keeps infrastructure and applications in the state that is wanted.

**Future Effects:** GitOps makes distribution easier and encourages building infrastructure that is version-controlled. It makes it easier for the development and operations teams to work together and makes deployments safer and easier to check.

### CI/CD with security first

When making software, security is very important. In the future, cloud-based CI/CD will put security first from the start by adding automatic security testing, vulnerability scanning, and compliance checks to the CI/CD pipeline.

**Future Effects:** CI/CD techniques that put security first will help find and fix vulnerabilities early in the development process, which will lower the risk of security breaches. DevSecOps, which adds security to the CI/CD process, will become the standard.

### Multiple cloud CI/CD

More and more businesses are using multicloud plans to avoid being locked into one vendor and get the most out of the best features from different cloud providers. Multicloud CI/CD pipelines make it easy to launch apps to multiple cloud platforms.

Multi cloud CI/CD will become more common in the future as businesses look for freedom and

redundancy. As time goes on, tools and systems will improve that make managing multicloud deployments easier.

### Unchangeable Hardware

Immutable infrastructure sends infrastructure in a state that can't be changed after it's been made. When changes need to be made, new infrastructure is built, tested, and put into use. This keeps things consistent and stops configuration drift.

**Effects on the Future:** Because it is reliable and predictable, immutable infrastructure will become more common. CI/CD pipelines will be made to build and handle infrastructure that can't be changed, which will allow for quick scaling and rolling back.

### Pipelines for Infrastructure as Code (IaC)

Infrastructure as Code (IaC) lets developers use code to describe and control infrastructure. IaC stages will be added to future CI/CD processes, which will allow infrastructure resources to be automatically set up and scaled.

**Future Effects:** IaC pipelines will give us more control and visibility over changes to infrastructure. This will cut down on mistakes made when setting things up by hand and speed up the process of giving apps resources.

### Automation Driven by AI

More and more, CI/CD jobs will be automated with the help of artificial intelligence (AI) and machine learning. AI algorithms can find the best deployment methods, guess what problems might happen, and suggest ways to make things run better.

**Future Effects:** Automation powered by AI will make CI/CD more reliable and efficient. AI-powered tools will likely become an important part of testing, deploying, and allocating resources in the best way.

### CI/CD Based on Events

CI/CD processes that are event-driven act on certain things, like code commits, pull requests, or

changes to the infrastructure. When things change, these systems automatically take the right steps.

**Future Effects:** CI/CD pipelines that are driven by events will make software release more flexible and quick. They will make growth and self-healing possible automatically, so people won't have to do as much to fix problems.

### CI/CD with little or no code

Low-code and no-code development tools are making it easier to make apps. These platforms could be added to future CI/CD pipelines so that business users can help automate and release software.

**Future Effects:** No-code or low-code CI/CD pipelines will make software development more accessible by letting people who aren't developers help automate and launch apps. This can speed up the delivery of applications.

### Green CD/CI

Sustainability is turning into a very important issue. Green CI/CD techniques try to make software development less harmful to the environment by making better use of resources, switching to infrastructure that uses less energy, and lowering carbon emissions.

**Future Effects:** Green CI/CD will help companies reach their sustainability goals and encourage developers to make software that is good for the world. Companies will focus on building infrastructure that uses less energy and makes the best use of their resources.

### Monitoring and feedback in real time

In CI/CD pipelines, real-time tracking and feedback loops will be the norm. These methods will give you immediate information about how well an app is working and how the user is experiencing it, so you can make changes quickly.

**Effects on the Future:** Real-time monitoring will improve the quality of software, customer satisfaction, and the speed with which problems can be found and fixed. Automated reactions and alerts will become an important part of keeping the system healthy.

### Using Edge Computing Together

CI/CD processes will work with edge computing, which moves computation closer to the source of the data. In the future, pipelines will make it easy to send apps to edge devices and places.

**Future Effects:** Adding edge computing to CI/CD pipelines will make it possible to deliver

high-performance, low-latency apps to edge devices, which will make the user experience better in IoT and 5G situations.

### A blockchain for CI/CD to build trust and give information

Blockchain technology will be used to make CI/CD processes more trustworthy and open. It can keep permanent records of changes to code, approvals, and deployments, which makes people more accountable and protects data.

**Effects in the future:** CI/CD based on blockchain will make software delivery methods more trustworthy. It will be especially useful in controlled fields where openness and ease of auditing are very important.

The future of cloud-based CI/CD is full of new ideas, automation, and a constant drive to make software delivery better. Serverless computing, machine learning, and Kubernetes-native CI/CD are some of the new technologies that will make it easier and faster to build and launch software applications. CI/CD pipelines will also be strong, efficient, and able to adapt to changing needs if security, sustainability, and real-time tracking are emphasized more. As businesses continue to use cloud-based CI/CD to stay ahead of the competition, it will be important to keep up with these trends in the constantly changing world of software development.

www.ingramcontent.com/pod-product-compliance
Lightning Source LLC
LaVergne TN
LVHW011938070526
838202LV00054B/4705